THE
RED
APPLES
WAY

Praise For *The RED APPLES Way*

"Marc hid some great advice in cheese so I could take the medicine I needed to hear. Business owners, entrepreneurs, and executive leadership alike will find actionable insights mixed with entertaining insider stories! Want to start a business? Read this first. Want to make an impact? Read this first."

—**Mary Nell Westbrook**, EVP, Chief Marketing & Communications Officer, Agiliti

"Real-world experience through a delightful and informative read. Each chapter of *The RED APPLES Way* builds on the core values with an anecdote and a quip to bring home the point. With each story, the reader is drawn into the analogy, gaining new insight and knowledge to apply in their own business and personal life."

—**Dr. Shelly Gerig**, Faculty Instructor; B.A.S., Leadership Program

THE

—RED—
APPLES
—WAY—

How Nine Core Values
Transformed A Business
Founded On *Fear & Desperation*
Into One Of *Passion & Purpose*

MARC ROBERTZ-SCHWARTZ

INDIE BOOKS
INTERNATIONAL

THE **RED APPLES** WAY
How Nine Core Values Transformed A Business Founded On
Fear & Desperation Into One Of Passion & Purpose

ISBN 13: 978-1-966168-58-4

Designed by Melissa Farr, Back Porch Creative, LLC

INDIE BOOKS INTERNATIONAL®, INC.
2511 WOODLANDS WAY
OCEANSIDE, CA 92054
www.indiebooksintl.com

Table Of Contents

Getting To The Core

We all have personal values. They are what define us and how we choose to live our lives. However, few of us live our lives while outright promoting our values. To do so might be perceived as arrogant, egotistical, or even indoctrinating. Individually, if we're even aware of our values, we tend to express them more subtly, through our actions and by surrounding ourselves with others who share our values.

On the other hand, business should also have values. Those should be clear, concise, and shared both loudly and proudly.

As someone who has worked with hundreds of businesses, companies, and organizations, I can tell you that while most do have values, they fall short in both articulation and implementation. That's where the problems begin.

Your company's values are your defining "DNA." They set the tone and standard for everything you do, everything you stand for, and should act as your guide for nearly every decision you make. Your company's values should be applied to the clients and customers you work with, the people you hire, the services you offer, and even how you grow and develop your business.

A lack of clear and concise direction is like getting on the road and driving to a place you've never been without a map. Sure, you may get there, eventually. You may even stumble onto a shorter, or more scenic, route; but I would argue that without that map, greater danger and the chance of wrong turns and frustrations await.

You're a few paragraphs in and may be thinking, "My business has core values."

Countless clients have told me they have company values, which leads me to a series of follow-up questions:

- Can you articulate them for me, right here, right now?
- If we called your receptionist or warehouse manager on the phone, could *they* articulate the company's values?
- How do you broadcast your values across your organization, as well as to your customers, vendors, stakeholders, and other strategic partners?
- What role do your core values play in holding your company focused and accountable?

As the founder of a nationally honored marketing agency, I certainly made my share of entrepreneurial mistakes. For me, the values of my newly formed company lived in my head. They served as a vague idea of how I thought I wanted this new company to be known. When I first started out as a bootstrapped staff of one, that was fine. But as the company grew, it was critical that I got those values out of my head and embedded into the culture of the company.

The concrete development and public proclamation of the RED APPLES core values marked one of the most critical milestones along the company's fifteen-year journey. Identifying and articulating who we were, what we stood for, and our commitment to those values provided unimaginable levels of focus, growth, and financial success.

Perhaps those results represent your company's aspirations as well. Why wouldn't they?

This is probably also a good time to distinguish what we're talking about in a book about core values.

Typically, a business or organization will focus on its mission, vision, brand, and core values. To oversimplify things, I would offer the following:

Mission statement: A clear and concise statement of an entity's purpose, often describing what it does, how it does it, and, generally, its reason for existence. This tends to be worded in the present tense. Common thinking is that the mission statement is a one- or two-sentence proclamation. *This book is not about that.*

Vision statement: The vision statement is just that, the entity's vision of the future, including its goals and aspirations. Clear and concise vision statements are also brief and to the point. *This book is not about that, either.*

Brand: This one is a bit more complicated and more debatable. However, I believe an entity's brand (even your own personal brand) is largely determined by the perceptions created by its customers, clients, and stakeholders. Brand is largely driven by image, based on the experiences it creates. *This book is a little bit about that.*

Core values: An entity's core values are the guiding principles that form the foundation of how it wishes to conduct itself. These values should be used to both influence decisions as well as to hold the entity and its people accountable for its actions based on its established values. When executed properly and consistently, the core values lead to a culture that supports the mission and vision. An important objective of the core values is to aid in establishing a brand that reflects the business entity in both perception and reality. While some would suggest that there should be three to seven core values, there is no magic number. What *is* important, is that they are memorable and actionable, primarily for the entity's staff, starting from the top of the organizational chart. That is why I created the RED APPLES core values as an acronym, with the intention of making it easier to remember all nine of them. *That is entirely what this book is about.*

CHAPTER 1

But First, The Back Story

For the first twenty years of my professional career, I worked in both affiliate and owned-and-operated television stations up and down the East Coast, from Maine to Miami. As you move through this book, you'll find many of the anecdotes and "interstitials" are derived from some pretty extraordinary experiences during those years, from celebrity interactions, to a horrific helicopter crash, and bosses, as well as coworkers, who shaped me (whether they intended to, realized it, or not).

One influential person was Don Browne, president and general manager of WTVJ—at the time, the NBC-owned television station in Miami. As his vice president of creative services, he and I had a very challenging relationship. However, I have to admit that he was one of the more influential people I had the opportunity to work with; we had some great experiences, some not so great, and others I swore I would never repeat.

I bring Don up this early because one of his favorite expressions was,

---

"In order to know where you're going, you have to know where you've been."

While a similar phrase is credited to Maya Angelou, he will forever be the person I attribute it to. With that philosophy in mind, I chose March of 2008 as my jumping point to begin the story that would eventually lead to *The RED APPLES Way*.

Don Browne and me at the groundbreaking for the new NBC6 broadcast facility in Miramar, FL, an interesting juxtaposition of our relationship

March 2008 marked my fifth anniversary with The Villages Media Group. For those of you who are unfamiliar, The Villages is a massive, active lifestyle, senior community in central Florida, about an hour north of Orlando. In 2003, when I was first recruited away from WFOR, the CBS television station in Miami, The Villages had an impressive population of about 50,000 people, spanning three adjacent counties.

At the time of this writing, the population is estimated to be more than triple that amount and still growing.[1]

A couple of months prior to my hiring, I received a call from an unknown number and instinctively sent it to voicemail. A while later, I played it back. It was from the head of human resources at The Villages—a place I had never heard of—asking if I would be open to talking about potentially coming on board as the general manager (GM) of their twenty-four-hour cable channel, VNN (The Villages News Network).

It had long been both a desire and goal of mine to be a GM of a television station, but I was told repeatedly that I either needed extensive TV advertising sales experience or previous general manager experience to even be considered. This reminded me a lot of when I was in college, interviewing for waiter positions at restaurants and being told they would only hire people with previous server experience. Ah yes, the old conundrum—how does one gain experience if no one is willing to hire someone without experience?

The job as GM at VNN seemed like it would be a wise way to earn those "GM stripes" and in three to five years, I could parlay that experience into getting back into mainstream local television somewhere as a general manager.

Press the fast-forward button to March 2008 when I approached my boss, the director of The Villages Media Group, and explained that my wife had been offered a buyout package from her employer. "I know there are no guarantees, but I just wanted to share that with you and get a sense of my future here," I explained. I will never forget his reply; it was short and to the point. "As long as I have a job, my man, you have a job."

I left his office with a degree of confidence that my family would be OK. Honestly, not a high degree of confidence, but enough. For those who recognize this point on the timeline, early 2008 was when the economy was starting to show some cracks while early prognosticators were warning of a potential "significant economic adjustment."

Five months after that conversation, I returned to work from a weeklong cruise. Two days after my return, my boss came to my office in the early afternoon and uttered the phrase I had been taught so well as an executive with hiring and firing responsibilities. "Today is your last day at The Villages."

We were trained to never give explanations, apologies, or anything else that could be used later in litigation or while filing for unemployment. I thought perhaps at my level, I might get more than the corporate line.

"I don't understand," I said.

"Today is your last day at The Villages," he repeated.

Did I do something wrong? Was it the economy, which was now showing some frightening signs of what was yet to come? I pressed for more and got nowhere until he offered, "You don't have to leave right away, but you do have to be out by the end of the day." That seemed pretty "right away" to me, but as it turned out, three other members of my team had already been let go and escorted from the building without my knowledge.

Here's my point—and my confession. I was miserable for the months leading up to that day. It had become an exhausting routine of navigating multiple unrealistic and ever-changing demands, politics (national and within the organization), and my determination to protect my small team of five from what seemed like a constant onslaught of undeserving attacks.

The signs were everywhere. It hurt to get up and go to work, and I dreaded practically every meeting and assignment. It went from the high point—in which I was regarded as an invaluable member of The Villages leadership team, even being nicknamed "Coolness" by the chief operating officer—to becoming a daily punching bag with no clear indication as to why. I hung in there and soldiered through, as driven and determined as I was the first day I arrived, never wanting to give anyone a reason to terminate me or any member of my team. I did this in part because I was very well compensated, enjoyed some unique perks and experiences (more on that later), and I was the primary source of income for our family, while my wife—after taking that buyout package—worked to get her boutique public relations and communications agency established.

In other words, The Universe had been lacing up its boots, but I had not yet been introduced to the ways of The Universe to be able to see it. It took a long, bitter while, but as I look back, I realize The Universe was giving me every opportunity to do what I knew in my gut was the right thing to do—look for another job. However, overwhelmed with complacency, even in the face of daily frustrations and the impact on both my mental and physical health, it took The Universe finally kicking me in the ass, in the form of being let go, to wake me up.

And this is where the story really begins. As an "accidental entrepreneur," I've been asked many times what gave me the courage to start my own company during the worst economic period in decades. I initially tapped into my corporate and media background to provide a crafted, nuanced, and diplomatic response. Over time, I became more comfortable with the truth. In fact, it wasn't courage at all. It was *"fear and desperation."* No one was hiring, let alone relocating, six-figure marketing and media executives as the economy was crashing on every front. I had a family, a mortgage, and a responsibility to do something—quickly.

About thirty days later, right after Thanksgiving, I started marketing a unique start-up concept—a local network of doctors' offices that would subscribe to being featured every month in an hour-long medical video program, *Hometown Health*. I had my first client in two weeks, put out our first of over 150 consecutive episodes in March 2009, and was modestly profitable within the first six months. I owe a great deal of our early production agility to the (now divorced) husband and wife who became my freelance production team. He was part of the group that got laid off with me on that fateful day a few months earlier. She had previously worked for me at VNN, and even though she and I had a very uncomfortable parting of ways, we were now all in the same boat—needing to generate income.

Over the next fifteen years, this little start-up company would expand the number of employees and office space, along with our capabilities and offerings. We would drive revenue and profitability, while winning a humbling number of both industry and community awards, including the 2012 International Incubator Business of the Year award (nontechnical sector) from the National Business Incubation Association. But, equally important, we did all of this while making a significant and lasting impact on the community we called home.

Initially incorporated as Hometown Health TV, LLC, we rebranded in 2014 as Red Apples Media to reflect a more diverse marketing agency and production company. In addition to a new name, RED APPLES would also become the acronym for the nine core values that served as my personal and professional blueprint for a company that was founded out of "*fear and desperation*," but would eventually transform into one of "*passion and purpose*."

Chamber of Commerce ribbon-cutting at Red Apples Media's most recent office (that's me with the scissors)

On the surface, these nine values may appear to be obvious to some. To others, you may struggle with how to apply them to your life, family, department, team, business, or organization. The reality is, you may choose to adjust and adapt the RED APPLES core values to your specific needs, having been inspired by what they stand for. On the other hand, you should also feel free to adopt any or all of them, as-is. My hope is that you will find a way to embrace as few as five of the nine, to help advance your trajectory toward success.

Before we dive in, I want to thank you in advance for indulging me in some stories of my past, which are scattered throughout. All true, generally relevant, and each intended to entertain a bit between the explanations of the core values. In the TV world, we would call these "interstitials"—the short features that break up the primary programming. Think in terms of *Schoolhouse Rock!*, in between your favorite Saturday morning cartoons. If you know the reference, you and I are going to be just fine throughout the remainder of this book.

CHAPTER 2

Respect The Universe (A Prelude)

While I plotted out the values that would be represented by each letter of RED APPLES, the first one came immediately, serving as the catalyst for the entire exercise: Respect The Universe.

As mentioned in the introduction, my path leading up to the launch of Hometown Health TV, LLC, was lined with influences and signs from The Universe. Nearly all of which I did not see, did not understand, or was determined to either ignore or dismiss.

Mostly, I was not yet dialed into the role of The Universe in my life. That has since changed, and while cliché, I can honestly say that awareness and acceptance of The Universe has been a game changer for me, as well as an indisputable factor in the rapid success of Red Apples Media. While this core value serves as the most important to me, both personally and professionally, it is the one that is most difficult for people to embrace and adopt.

Respecting The Universe requires a high level of self-awareness and confidence. It demands that you release your iron-fist grip for control, not only over your own life in general, but more importantly, the things we have little if any actual control over. This is where I often start to get raised eyebrows as I share this abstract philosophy. The skepticism is usually driven by variations of, "Yeah, but . . ."

We'll get into some of these later, but what I've come to understand and appreciate (sometimes, counterintuitively) is that respecting The Universe also comes with three critical stipulations:

1. You can't negotiate with The Universe.
2. You can't time The Universe.
3. You can't beat The Universe.

Of all the core values I will share, this is the first, the most impactful, the one I am most passionate about, and the one that requires the most amount of engagement and trust.

So, as I prepare to leave you hanging until the final chapters, in which I will pull everything together and take you on a deep dive into the ways of The Universe, let me quickly answer the most frequent question that comes from this conversation:

Q: "How did you first come to realize the impact of The Universe?"
A: "At a baseball game—in Pittsburgh."

CHAPTER 3

INTERSTITIAL

Bangor Or Bust!

During spring break of my senior year at the University of Florida (UF), my parents treated my younger brother and me to a family trip to Hawaii as an early celebration of my graduation. (UF is where I would earn a degree in Telecommunications Management, from the College of Journalism and Communications, and gain internship experience as a promotions producer at WCJB, the ABC TV station in Gainesville, Florida.) Knowing I would be visiting Hawaii, I mailed letters to each of the TV station general managers, requesting an interview while I was in Honolulu (yes, this was before email was an option).

Remarkably, one called me a few weeks later. Jim Matthews, the general manager of KITV, invited me to stop by for an informal interview during my trip. One of my college roommates was from Hawaii and she was all in when I first told her about it. She started spewing all kinds of information, valuable phrases, tips, and advice. However, our toughest topic of conversation centered on what I should wear for the interview. Did I really want to schlep a suit that would be worn for about thirty minutes on a weeklong trip to Hawaii?

In the middle of the afternoon, I left my family on the beach, headed up to the room to shower, got dressed, and took a cab to KITV, the ABC station in Honolulu.

As I entered Mr. Matthews's office, in my gray suit, white shirt, and a paisley power tie, the man who could be my first boss stood up from behind the desk, wearing khakis and a Hawaiian shirt. He extended his hand to shake mine and the first words out his mouth were, "Nice suit. Someone didn't do his homework about what to wear on a Friday in Hawaii."

All decked out in my best (and only) suit and paisley tie
for my interview at KITV in Hawaii

"Respectfully," I began, as I shared a firm handshake, "my college roommate is from Hawaii, and she warned me I would be overdressed. But I thought it would be presumptuous of me to adopt the spirit of aloha, being a haole and all." He smiled, laughed, and said, "Yeah, guess you did do your homework."

By the time we were done, he offered me a job, but it came with a caution. He gave me a week to get back to him, strongly encouraging me to do my homework before deciding. First, he wanted me to understand the value of the salary he was offering me, which would have been a lot in Gainesville, but after researching, I'd learn it was barely livable on the island of Oahu. To throw an additional wrench into things, my research revealed that if I brought my black Labrador, Nina, with me to Hawaii, she would have to quarantine for several months (an effort to minimize animal disease, rabies, and parasites, from coming to the island from the mainland).[2]

A few days later, I also received an offer from WABI, the CBS television station in Bangor, Maine, but for half the salary that Matthews had offered. With the cost of living and the quarantine driving my decision, I was Bangor bound. Matthews was not only understanding, he encouraged me to stay in touch.

I had practiced saying "*Huh-wuh-ee*" like a native for weeks. Now I had to properly pronounce the name of my new home, right out of college, "*Bang-gore*."

That summer, WABI had acquired the syndication rights to *The Cosby Show*. The station paid a lot of money to make it a cornerstone of its Monday-through-Friday programming to draw viewers. Shortly after the launch on our station, Bill Cosby came to Portland, Maine, to do a stand-up show. It was during the time of Cosby mania and the arena was sold out. As a partner station, we had given away tickets to some viewers who won on-air contests. Additionally, the general manager of the station brought some of the larger advertisers. I was tasked with driving the marked station van to the arena and parking it right out front, for high visibility and promotional awareness as people arrived at the event. As I was leaving the station, I grabbed some of the marketing posters that had been sent to us. The poster featured Cosby and the bold text, "The Cosby Show, Five Times A Week."

Maybe if I got lucky, I could get them autographed for future giveaways or advertiser gifts.

Unfamiliar with the route (pre-GPS) and underestimating the traffic, by the time I arrived and parked the station van, the performance had started. Cosby was in the round, and already had command of the audience. The station's seats were near the edge of the stage, so I put my head down, rolled posters under my arm, and headed to my seat.

I suddenly noticed Cosby had stopped talking. I kept walking. There was a silence followed by a curious roar of laughter.

Out of the corner of my eye, I saw myself on the jumbo screens that hung over the stage. As I looked up, Cosby was standing at the edge of the stage, staring down at me.

He announced into the microphone, "You're late." As the audience exploded with laughter, I felt my legs weakening, my heart racing, and my face filling with blood.

"Sorry," I offered.

"Why are you late? Did you not know you were coming here tonight until fifteen minutes ago?"

"I was parking the van."

More laughter and a smile from Cosby.

"What's under your arm?" he asked.

"Posters."

"Of what?"

"You."

"Can I see?" Cosby asked.

I was about ready to throw up, but was in no position to say no, or try to outwit Bill Cosby with some clever comeback. I reached up to the edge of the stage and unrolled the posters at his feet. Cosby bent down, picked one up and held it for the entire arena to see.

The place erupted; I was ready to go to my seat, but Cosby wasn't done with me yet. He pressed on.

"What were you planning to do with these?" he asked, as if he was teeing up one of his famous life-lesson lectures to his TV son, Theo.

Timidly, I answered, "I was hoping to get them autographed."

Bill Cosby, standing about five feet over me just from the height of the stage, in addition to his six-plus additional feet of stature, looked down at me, paused for a beat, held the microphone to his mouth, and uttered one his most famous lines from his stand-up routine, "Noah."

"Riiiiiiiiiiiiiiiiiiight."

The arena was filled with deafening laughter and applause. He turned his back and picked up from exactly where he left off in his routine before I interrupted it. I rolled up the posters and finally made it to my seat.

Now just a few seats away from my immediate boss, the TV station manager, he leaned over and said to me, "You couldn't have said something about watching The Cosby Show five nights a week on Channel 5?"

At the end of the show, one of Cosby's staff caught me as we were getting up from our seats and informed me, "Mr. Cosby would like two of the posters for a couple of his young guests. If you give them to me, he will sign all of them and I will bring the others back to you."

Only five of those signed posters exist and I still have one today, unfortunately stashed in the back of a closet. Enough said.

Around the six-month mark, I saw an announcement in one of the TV industry magazines that Jim Matthews had left Hawaii and was now the general manager at WJKS, the ABC TV station in Jacksonville, Florida. I wrote him another letter.

Mr. Matthews called me about two weeks later and asked if I would like to join him in Jacksonville as a promotions producer. I packed up the rented trailer, and with Nina in the passenger seat for the long drive, headed back to the Sunshine State.

A few months later, ABC's *Good Morning America* hit the road for a series of live morning shows around the country. Jacksonville was one of their first stops. Our station assisted with much of the production and on-site support. One of my jobs was to hold up cue cards after the live show was over, so that Charles Gibson and Joan Lunden could record promotional "wild lines" for some of the ABC stations that would also be hosting them in the days to come. Portland, Maine, was one of their next stops, so they were recording promo lines for all of the ABC TV stations in Maine.

Charles Gibson and Joan Lunden on location in Jacksonville, FL

We were chugging along just fine. Charlie and Joan were one-take pros, until:

Charlie: "Good morning, America, I'm Charles Gibson."

Joan: "And I'm Joan Lunden. We invite you to watch us live when we visit Portland, right here on WVII—ABC7, Bangger."

Charlie didn't skip a beat.

Charlie: "And bang *him*, too!"

The whole crew burst out laughing. Joan didn't know what was so funny. Charlie explained he didn't think she correctly pronounced "Bangor." Joan insisted she did.

The producer asked out loud, "Does anyone know for sure?"

I replied, "It's pronounced *Bang-gore*."

"Are you sure?" Joan asked the kid holding the cue cards.

"Positive."

Me and Nina at one of her favorite places, Atlantic Beach, FL

CHAPTER 4

Excellence In Everything. Period.

T here is an expression you've probably heard, "Fake it till you make it."

I hate this expression. It makes me insane. To me, it's even worse if people are faking it while on someone else's dime. In other words, would you dine at a pizza parlor where the cooks were first trying to figure out how to make pizza while charging you for the pie you sat and ate? Sure, restaurants have "soft openings," where they work out kinks and groom their staff and adjust procedures in operational environments before opening to the public. Typically, you know this ahead of time, preparing yourself to be understanding and patient with any shortcomings. This is why you rarely pay full price, if at all, for the experience of a "soft opening."

I decided early on that Red Apples Media would *never* subscribe to a "fake it till you make it" mentality, especially with a paying client. In other words, excellence in everything. Period.

I had an expectation of everyone we hired that they would always put forth their best effort and always take a proactive approach to raising his or her own level of excellence by learning, exploring, pushing their boundaries, and navigating through comfort zones. Those who were most successful and most valuable at Red Apples Media were those who bought into this with little, if any, nudging. Not everyone did. Upon reflection, failure for an employee to embrace a commitment to unwavering excellence probably led to more partings (their choice or ours) than any other infraction or shortcoming.

Yes, mistakes happen. I don't mind mistakes the first time they happen. I may even have patience if a variation of the initial mistake occurs a second time. But there is only one thing that gets me more frustrated than mistakes, and that's apathy or lack of ownership of a mistake.

The formula is simple:

Mistake + Ownership + Learning =
Not making the mistake again

But sometimes it's not just about a mistake. Sometimes it's about not reaching a level of capability, also known as "laziness." Remember Don Browne from WTVJ? He had another expression: "There are three kinds of people. Those who are willing and able. Those who are willing and not able. Those who are able but not willing."

At Red Apples Media, typically a video editor and a producer worked together on each project. During one period, we had a video editor who made a habit of presenting mediocre projects for me to review. Initially, I chalked it up to him being on a learning curve or lacking confidence in the work that I believed he was capable of. My approach was to always hold the producer ultimately accountable for the project, as it was their responsibility to oversee all the elements (and effort) that went into the final production.

As my frustration grew with the frequency of the changes that had to be made, or the suggestions needed to enhance projects so they were worthy of submitting to a client for review and approval, the producer shared that her editor told her that all he had to do was "get the project to about 80 percent and then Marc would polish it before it was sent out."

Eighty percent is not a commitment to excellence.

Of course, my first thought was whether that meant I only had to pay him 80 percent of his hourly rate.

Unfortunately, this person fell into the "able but not willing" category and, frankly, there is no room for that kind of person in any organization.

On the other hand, I beam when I think about the young woman I hired at Red Apples Media, who had no specific experience in what we were doing but had a work ethic that I could not let escape.

We were hiring an administrative assistant and she was one of two finalists. I gave the job to the other candidate, but in breaking the news, I explained that if she trusted me and was willing to take a leap of faith, I wanted to carve out a position within Red Apples for her. I was drawn to her diligence and communication during the interview process, and I had a strong hunch she would subscribe to "Excellence In Everything."

As you can probably guess, the admin hire failed about four months into her tenure. On the other hand, my on-the-fly hire became a critical and trusted member of the team.

Together, we turned someone who was willing but not able into someone who became able because she was willing.

In ranking my people-management shortcomings over the course of my career, one of the top three would be giving people too much time to make course corrections, with the hope of salvaging someone (and their livelihood). Part of this mindset came from a philosophy at The Villages, "Groom before you broom."

Having managed hundreds of people during my career, I can count on one hand the number of people where that strategy paid off. Unfortunately, the scale tips too far with the weight of those I kept around longer than I should have, almost always at the expense of the rest of the organization. Sometimes that manifested as resentment from others on the team who were pulling their own weight, plus the additional weight of some of the underperformers. It almost always created stress and tension in the office with eyes on me, waiting to see how long it would take for me to enforce this core value and hold those who did not subscribe to it, accountable.

Jeremy Foley, legendary athletic director at the University of Florida, has been widely quoted with some variation of,

---

"What should be done eventually, must be done immediately."[3]

Perhaps this sounds harsh on the surface; but in other words, core values are worthless if they are not woven into the culture of the organization and used for both reward and accountability.

Along the way, some challenged what "excellence" really meant.

In one off-site midyear strategy meeting with the Red Apples staff, I got into a very—let's call it *spirited*—conversation with a member of the team who insisted that excellence could never be achieved, and that striving for it was a recipe for failure. I suggested he was confusing excellence with perfection.

To illustrate my point, I had pulled together the quantifiable year-to-date costs associated with having to fix errors. These included examples such as having to reprint a billboard vinyl because an error was found after it had been printed (yes, the client signed off before going to print, having missed the error as well, but the responsibility was ultimately ours and we "ate the cost" of the reprint). Other errors were harder to quantify, like the on-the-clock time spent having to re-edit a video due to sloppy edits, poorly mixed audio, or graphics errors.

Deadlines, too many projects in the pipeline, distractions, and thinking someone else should have caught the error, were frequent excuses. Someone earlier in my TV career used to lament, "We never have the time to do it right, but we always make the time to do it over."

For the first eight months of that particular year, quantifiable errors cost Red Apples Media about $14,000. I'm not sure if you think that number is a lot or a little, but for perspective, it represented about 15 percent of our net revenue at the time (I did not share that percentage with the staff).

Sensing apathy regarding the amount, I explained that if I divided $14,000 by 2,080 (the total number of hours a full-time, forty-hour-per-week employee would work during a calendar year), that equated to about $6.75 per hour. Divided by the six employees at the time (not including me), errors now equated, on average, to about one dollar per hour per employee, or nearly $2,100 each per year in additional income if we could eliminate the errors. It was a pledge I was happy to make.

Suddenly there was a tangible incentive to strive for "excellence in everything. Period."

As the owner of Red Apples Media, it was always my responsibility to make the phone call (never an email) to the client whenever we made a significant error and had to own up to it. Even though I could have pointed to the client's sign-off as an excuse to pass along the expense for the error, I never did. The RED APPLES Way demanded excellence, and anything that fell short of that was ours to learn from, fix, and avoid repeating.

The bottom line is that clients, bosses, friends, and family don't want excuses. They want reliability, understanding things may not always be perfect. They want to know that you care enough about the value that's been entrusted in you to come through with consistency—a commitment to excellence. It doesn't matter whether you're compensated by a paycheck, a verbal or written "thank you," a peck on the cheek from your loved one, or if the only compensation is your own personal satisfaction for having integrity.

Excellence is the effort, perfection is the potential.

CHAPTER 5

INTERSTITIAL

Madonna Did What?

I have shared this story many times verbally over the years, but never in writing. My hope is that it will convey to you just as well by reading it as it has for those who have heard me tell it. Either way, there's a lesson to be learned.

Back at WTVJ in Miami, I was working on something at my desk when our department administrative assistant came into my office and explained, "There is an elderly woman on the phone who wants to speak to the station voice."

The Creative Services department became the default transfer whenever the switchboard was unable to decipher what the person was calling about. But in this case, it was certainly transferred to the right department.

"I don't understand," I replied, looking at her quite perplexed.

"I don't know. She said she heard something very offensive while she was watching [one of the morning talk shows] and wants to talk to the voice."

OK, now I'm getting somewhere. My sense was that she was referring to our professional voiceover person who announces the script copy we send him to read, likely to promote something that is coming up later that day on the news. The dude literally just records from somewhere, probably wearing shorts and flip-flops, and sends back an audio file of exactly what we wrote for him to announce.

At this point, I had a lot of options for the assistant:

- "Take her name and number and I'll get back to her—or not."
- "Why don't you handle this crackpot?"
- "Sounds like a news thing. Transfer her to the newsroom and let them deal with it."
- "Just leave her on hold until she hangs up."
- "Go ahead and put her through."

I opted for the last option.

I answered the phone and recall the conversation with the elderly female viewer going like this:

Me: "Hi, this is Marc. How can I help you?"

Her: "Are you the voice I hear on the TV?"

Me: "No ma'am. I believe you're referring to the announcer and he does not physically work in our building. How can I help you?"

Her: "I don't think you can."

Me: "Well, ya got me, so try me. What's going on?"

Her: "Who are you?"

Me: "My name is Marc. I'm the vice president of creative services here at NBC6. The announcer works for me and my team."

Her: (pause) "I don't understand any of what you just said, but I am offended by what I heard this morning on your TV station."

Me: "What did you hear?"

Her: "The voice said, 'Madonna is seen with a *black guy*. We'll tell you why, tonight at six.' Why does it matter what color the man was? It was horribly racist!"

Me: "Ma'am, that doesn't sound right to me. There must be some confusion."

Her: "I know what I heard!"

Me: "Let's do this: Can you please give me your name and number, let me dig into this, and I'll get back to you?"

Her: "No, you won't. I'll never hear back from you again. You're just trying to get rid of me."

Me: "How about we do this: You give me your name and number, I'll give you my boss's name and number, and if you don't hear back from me in thirty minutes, you can call back and complain to my boss."

We swapped information and I dove in, the clock ticking.

My first call was to my promotions producer, asking her what we were promoting for the news that night. The only part I remember her telling me was, ". . . oh, and something about Madonna being seen last night in South Beach."

"That one. What's the script say?"

She pulled up the script on her computer and read it to me over the phone: "(blah, blah, blah) . . . and, Madonna is seen at a South Beach club with a black eye—we'll tell you why, tonight at six."

Are you kidding me?

Apparently, Madonna had been accidentally punched in the eye by her toddler and had a shiner to show for it.

A black *eye*, not a black *guy*. But say that out loud to yourself and you can certainly see where there could be some unfortunate confusion without the correct enunciation.

With a good twenty minutes to spare, I called the viewer back and explained to her what the announcer really said, and that I could absolutely understand the confusion.

She let out a hysterical cackle that forced me to pull the phone away from my ear as she laughed for a good ten seconds. Once she gained her composure, she thanked me for looking into it and calling her back, and she shared how embarrassed she felt.

I thanked her for bringing it to our attention. Surely if *she* heard it that way, others must have as well.

It was a simple (and entertaining) gesture that took about fifteen minutes of my day, from first call transfer to final resolution. And while it cleared up the specific concern for her, more importantly, she felt heard and respected by the effort.

I made her day. She made our day. We gained a viewer for life. I gained a story, and a lesson I have shared dozens of times since.

Before we return to your regularly scheduled core values, let me share two more quick phone stories, if I may.

For the life of me, I will never understand how the Red Apples Media voicemail wound up with an overnight message from a woman who kept repeating, "OK Google . . . OK Google . . . What is the alcohol content of a Red Apple Ale? It says I'm offline . . . Check your connection . . . OK Google, what . . . is . . . the alcohol . . . content . . . in . . . a . . . Red . . . Apple . . . Ale?"

Gotta love it when your website's SEO outranks a national brand.

I did not return that call.

In early 2020, a company with a similar name, Red Apple Media (singular apple), acquired storied New York radio station WABC. For the next few months, our Red Apples Media in Florida would get calls from people who wanted to advertise, complain about programming, or ask whether school would be cancelled for snow, among other interesting inquiries.

It took me a few days to figure out why we were suddenly getting these odd calls for a New York radio station (which I grew up listening to as a kid in New Jersey). I answered every call, and by asking a few questions, quickly tracked down the source of the confusion: lazy web searches.

But one call stood out to me. One morning I answered the phone, and it was a young man who was calling about the overnight switchboard operator position that he had applied for. He went on for about twenty seconds, telling me how great he would be for the job, that he was a night owl so an overnight shift would not be a problem, and that he was good on the phone and great with detail. It broke my heart to stop him after he shared that attention-to-detail "strength," and then break the news that he had called the wrong Red Apples Media. I wished him luck with the job search.

I will very rarely not take or not return a call. You just never know what The Universe dialed up for you.

CHAPTER 6

Deliver On Commitments, Overdeliver On Expectations

I f you ever run into my daughter, ask her what our lives are defined by, and I guarantee she will parrot back to you a philosophy I began sharing with her starting when she was around six years old (and have reminded her of many times over the years):

"Our lives are defined by two things:
the commitments we make,
and the integrity we have to keep them."

The *D* in the RED APPLES core values was my nod to that philosophy, without having either a *C* (commitment) or *I* (integrity) to work with in the acronym. So, to paraphrase: Deliver on commitments. Overdeliver on expectations.

I like to refer to this one as "the reality and the perception."

To make a commitment is to create a reality of expectation and delivery. It is almost always tangible.

"I will be on time for our meeting."

"I will make that deadline."

"I will deliver the project within the budget we discussed."

"I will pick you up from school on time."

"I will be there for your dance recital."

All of these are tangible, quantifiable, and will result in either a successful or failed commitment.

There are those who will say things like:

"I'll try to be on time."

"I should be able to meet the deadline."

"I'll see what I can do to stay within budget."

Those are not commitments. Those are soft suggestions of good intentions, at best.

The greater the commitment and the more extraordinary or unattainable it may seem to the person you're committing to, the greater the opportunity to overdeliver on their expectations.

It's sad when expectations are so low, simply because that person has been let down so many times that the commitment rings hollow. Red Apples Media built a reputation doing what other marketing and production companies failed to do, not to mention their failure to deliver in the manner and timeliness in which they said they'd do it. There were even occasions when a client was lured away by another agency and, I would say, 50 percent of the time, they found their way back to Red Apples. We had set the standard of expectation, and while others had a slick up-front pitch, the proof would be in the performance—or lack thereof.

To publicly state in our core values that Red Apples Media subscribes to "Excellence In Everything," is to set ourselves up to be held accountable to delivering on that commitment—both among ourselves, as well as by our clients, vendors, and community. It didn't matter whether we were generating revenue from you or not. A value is a value, under any and all circumstances.

On the other hand, think about the qualifying words we sometimes use when we speak to someone. Notice, in using qualifiers, the difference between committing versus waffling. Is it so unreasonable to say, "I *will* be on time for the meeting," versus "I'll *try* to be on time for the meeting"?

You determine what time to start the journey to the client meeting, whether driving thirty minutes away or walking thirty feet down the hall. Granted, you may not have anticipated the accident that stopped traffic along the way, but hopefully two things happened: (1) you immediately contacted the client to let them know where you were, what happened, and when you think you'll arrive; (2) you've already developed a reputation of reliability and integrity, and these rare circumstances are seen as anomalies and not reflective of your character.

When we first launched the *Hometown Health* program, we would often ask our medical clients, "What differentiates you from other practices?"

The answer was always (and I mean *always*) the same. Say it with me: "We are committed to treating our patients like family."

Assuming they liked their family, I can assure you that they rarely delivered on that commitment. In fact, having been a patient of a few of our medical clients, all I can say is, thank goodness I'm not a member of his/her family, if patient treatment was any indication.

Several come to mind who did deliver on their commitment of excellent communication before, during, and after the appointment; being courteous in how they spoke to me and the time they spent; being punctual with the appointment time; billing properly; and simply extending human courtesies from the moment I walked in until the time I walked out. These were the ones who would remain cornerstones of Red Apples Media's medical portfolio of clients long after COVID-19 shut down production of *Hometown Health*. Whether by chance, circumstance, or The Universe, we shared common values in how we did business and treated each other in our multilayered relationship.

I am reminded of one of our initial meetings with a potential internist and our pitch for him to join the *Hometown Health* network.

Because the meeting was set for lunchtime when the office closed to patients, I was asked to bring lunch for the physician I would be meeting with, as well as his staff. I was also warned to be on time, as he would only have thirty minutes for us. Bringing food to a medical office was a very common practice for medical and pharmaceutical reps from large companies, who were either trying to win—or keep—an office's business by delivering a catered meal using their corporate expense card. Free food is a powerful incentive for an office staff who are gatekeeping for barely more than minimum wage.

However, as a small business in our early stages with limited funds, this was both foreign and unexpected for me to be asked to provide lunch for a presentation about our marketing and production vehicle. By then, one other person had joined my staff, and I was training her to also do presentations for prospective medical practices. The two of us drove together, picked up two large pizzas, and headed over to the office, arriving about ten minutes ahead of our meeting time.

When we entered the waiting area, I was immediately struck by all the computer printed signs that completely covered the closed sliding-glass receptionist window.

You must pay your copay when you check in.

If you are later than thirty minutes, you will forfeit your appointment and be charged a fee.

Turn off the sound and ringer on your cell phone.

Do not knock on the glass. We know your there. (Their typo, not mine.)

Careful not to break any of the "window witch" rules, we sat down with the pizzas and waited. And waited. And waited, for about twenty minutes. We could hear people behind the glass. I even went up to the glass and without knocking on it said, "Excuse me? Anyone there?"

Finally, someone came out. She told me the doctor was running late and that she would take the pizzas back to the staff in the break room. No "Thank you," no "Would you like to join us?"

And then we waited. And waited some more. After forty-five minutes, I turned to my "wing woman" and said, "If he tells me he treats his patients like family, I'm going to slap him." OK, I wouldn't really. Nor did I ever find out whether he would say that or not.

After an hour, the afternoon patients started to come in for their appointments, so we got up and left. It was a forty-dollar waste of pizza, and our time. But two very valuable things came from that experience. I realized this office lacked the integrity to deliver on its commitments—never mind whether they would pay our invoices on time—if we had taken them on as a client. I also later learned that the physician was apparently twice divorced for cheating with a staff member, his staff was constantly turning over, and he had a two-star rating on one of the patient review websites for medical providers.

The Universe helped me dodge what I'm sure would have been a nightmare of a client relationship. After all, "Our lives are defined by two things: the commitments we make, and the integrity we have to keep them."

For me, the sheer delight of overdelivering has always been a motivator. In a society where we all live and die by online reviews, to read an unsolicited client review that includes the phrase "overdelivered," means a great deal—not only because we've exceeded their expectations, but because now they've perpetuated the expectation of overdelivery for anyone who reads that review.

Of course, there will be times where we simply cannot commit to something and hedging the action will be necessary. For me, as a daughter dad with a new company, being there for my daughter was a nonnegotiable commitment. In 2012, Hometown Health TV, LLC, won the International Incubator Business of the Year award (nontechnical sector) from the National Business Incubation Association. Imagine that. Little ole Hometown Health TV in Leesburg, Florida, beat out thousands of incubator-based businesses across the US and several other countries.

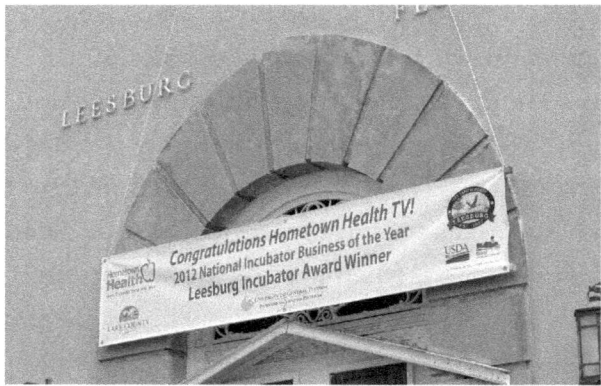

The city of Leesburg, FL celebrated our recognition with this large banner on the incubator building

With the award reception being held in Atlanta, my wife and I took our daughter out of school for two days to join us for the seven-hour drive north for the awards luncheon. Most kids would have just seen it as a day away from school, but I truly do believe my eleven-year-old daughter had a solid understanding and appreciation of the accomplishment and its magnitude. She, along with my wife, had been firmly strapped into the rollercoaster that I had been riding for the first three years of accidental entrepreneurship leading up to this.

Nearly every night, as we would recap our day over dinner, my daughter would ask, "Any new Hometown Health clients today, Daddy?"

It became a family celebration when we got one, or a support session when one didn't go my way. It was also interesting for me to realize over time how much we were all learning about the medical community, doctors, conditions, treatments, and breakthroughs. I think this also helped remove all fear of doctors that most kids her age would typically have.

During the awards luncheon, we were sitting at the head table when one of the board members from the National Business Incubation Association—a sweet, older, Southern woman—leaned over to my daughter and said with her perfect drawl, "*Now* you understand how hard your dad was working and why he had to miss so many of your things."

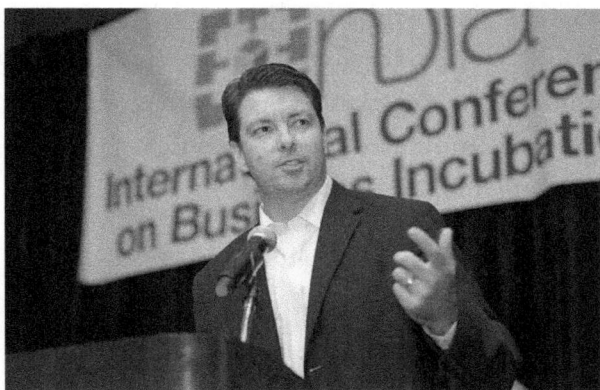

Accepting the 2012 Outstanding Incubator Client award in Atlanta, GA

I completely understood the well-intentioned comment and what she was suggesting, and I had hoped my daughter would respectfully smile and offer a "Yes, ma'am." She did not.

In a polite, matter-of-fact tone, she replied, "I can't think of anything he missed."

For me, that was the purest acknowledgement of delivering on my commitment to her.

Fortunately, or unfortunately—depending on what side of this statement you're on—there is a huge opportunity to differentiate yourself and your business in a culture that seems to be lacking in the area of commitment.

How many appointments have you scheduled, let's say, to have something checked at your home, and the service provider left you hanging for hours or even days?

How many times have you scheduled a potential employee for an interview, and they were a no-show?

How many times has someone told you they would get back to you and didn't?

See where I'm going with this?

Set your commitments at a level you know that you'll deliver on. Then, whenever possible, find a way to overdeliver. Beyond the core commitment, aim to work ahead of schedule, come in under budget, and throw a little something extra in. Few things make for a stronger service brand than commitments and integrity.

Just ask my daughter.

CHAPTER 7

INTERSTITIAL

The Joe Blow

Growing up in New Jersey, we were surrounded by Jets and Giants football fans. I can't recall ever really being a fan of either, although my dad has always been a die-hard Giants fan, through good times and dismal ones. I was more of a baseball kid—collecting cards (many of which my grandmother threw away during one of our moves; don't ask), listening to Yankee games on my AM radio with the single-wired earpiece (so my parents couldn't hear me listening to the night games). I even played for a few years during middle school.

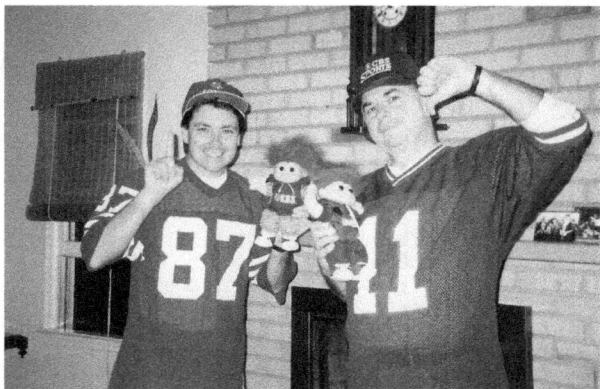

Growing up a Niners fan while my dad stayed true to his NY Giants

It wasn't until my mother's cousin (I guess that makes him my first cousin once removed), an executive with Levi Strauss in San Francisco, sent 49ers jerseys to me and my brother for our birthdays one year. I got (Joe) Montana, he got (Dwight) Clarke (which I borrowed for the photo on the previous page). We didn't know much about the Niners at that time, but we quickly caught on as it was during the early 1980s, known as the "golden years" of their success, with them winning the Super Bowl in 1982, 1985, and 1989.

It was a lonely time, being a Joe Montana fan in central New Jersey during the eighties, but I was all in.

I acquired an impressive collection of his trading cards throughout high school and even into college. As a matter of fact, I was at a college event in Tampa, staying at the same hotel the 49ers were staying for a game against the Buccaneers, and happened to be standing right next to Joe Montana when I checked in. Without any hesitation, I reached over the desk and grabbed the first piece of paper within my reach and asked if he would sign it. He did, without saying a word or even looking up at me, but I didn't particularly care—*I got my sports idol's autograph* (and still have it)!

When my wife and I first started dating, one of the first significant gifts she bought me was a second-year Joe Montana trading card, unable to afford his rookie card (understandably—we were still young and early in our careers, living paycheck-to-paycheck). It meant a great deal to me, and became a coveted addition to my collection of his various trading cards.

Skip ahead about three years and Joe's career with the 49ers was starting to wind down. An extremely talented quarterback named Steve Young took over for Montana, who had suffered an elbow injury that cost him most of the 1992 season. Niners fans saw the writing on the wall—Young was the future of San Francisco football.

Here's what I've been building to.

In March of 1993, I was working as a promotions producer at WBAL, the Baltimore CBS television station. I had become close with the primary sports anchor, Gerry Sandusky (no relation to the Penn State Sandusky investigations). WBAL was a sponsor of the Ed Block Courage Awards, an annual fundraising event that would honor one player from each NFL team. I was excited to learn that Montana would be the 49ers honoree, and all indications were that he would be attending the event.

In the days leading up to the event, I began to lobby Gerry to let me be part of the crew that was going to cover it. The problem was, WBAL was a "union shop" station. This meant, as a nonunion employee, I was extremely limited in what I could do and the equipment I could touch, even if he did allow me to tag along. He kept giving me diplomatic variations of, "Let's see what happens as we get closer."

You can't get much closer than the morning of the event when Gerry came to my desk and said something along the lines of, "OK, you got your wish."

Rumors started to swirl the night before that Montana had been traded by the 49ers to the Kansas City Chiefs. The idea that Joe Montana would play anywhere other than San Francisco would rock the NFL.

Gerry wanted to make absolutely sure that if Montana still came to the event, we would get him on tape responding to the trade rumors. He knew there were two ways into the venue; he had two camera guys and needed one more person to stick with the second camera, to cover the entry point that Gerry and his camera guy were not covering.

"You do one thing and one thing only," Gerry told me, knowing we were walking a very fine union line. "You ask him, 'Mr. Montana, can you comment on the rumors you've been traded to Kansas City?' that's all. You cannot freeze when you see him. No autographs. Nothing more than that question. You with me?"

Hell yeah, I was!

We arrived at the venue about an hour ahead of schedule, leaving nothing to chance that Montana might try to sneak in ahead of the media before the event started. We waited.

And waited some more.

My camera guy and I kept doing microphone checks. I kept checking the battery level on the microphone. No technical issue was going to torpedo my mission, damn it.

The longer we waited, the more crowded the entry became, as more guests arrived. I was surrounded by people with memorabilia from Notre Dame (Montana's college team) and the 49ers, salivating at the possibility of landing an autograph (so childish).

Suddenly—and I will never forget these twenty seconds of my life—one of the autograph hounds announces, "There's Joe!" I turned around and saw my childhood football idol walking toward me in a suit and tie, surrounded by some other people (no idea who they were, but they appeared to be security of some kind). As he got closer, I held the mic to my mouth and said, "Mr. Montana, can you comment on the rumors you've been traded to the Chiefs?" And then I thrust the microphone in his direction, following him in stride, body blocking the autograph seekers around me.

Just to recap, this is the guy whose jersey I had been wearing since the mid-eighties. I had amassed around 150 of his trading cards and dozens of his magazine covers. Heck, we were old buddies, dating back to that hotel interaction in Tampa.

Which is why, when he stopped, looked me in the eye, waved me off, and used some very inappropriate language in suggesting my next personal activity, I stood stunned as he walked off.

The camera guy zoomed out to reveal me, the camera shaking just enough to know that he was laughing behind the lens at the look on my face. Gerry would refer to this classic moment in sports journalism as "The Joe Blow Off" (or simply "The Joe Blow," as the story evolved over time).

Joe Montana waving off my question about his trade to the Chiefs

During Gerry's sportscast that night, he showed that clip repeatedly. It was great material, artistically produced, and masterfully interwoven throughout his coverage of Baltimore sports that evening. The clip always cut out before you could see me (that would probably have been the crossing of the union line, had I been seen on camera).

Yeah, I was the butt of some ribbing around the station for a few days afterward, and we both caught a little heat from the news director the next morning. But Gerry Sandusky—who, to this day, is one of the classiest people I've ever met in television—would never let me forget that night. This served as a valuable lesson, reminding me of the hazards associated with putting our idols too high on that pedestal in our minds.

Gerry Sandusky, a Baltimore sportscasting legend, on location at Camden Yards

CHAPTER 8

Anticipate Client Needs
And Opportunities

There is absolutely an art to being proactive: the ability to think ahead of those you're supporting—whether clients, coworkers, family or friends. Think about the feeling you had when someone proactively reached out to make sure you knew a favorite band was coming to town, that a product you often purchase was on sale, or even that a section of your lawn was starting to brown (there's a reason I threw that one in). At worst, you may have already been aware but appreciated the fact that someone took time from their schedule to not only think of you, but took the extra step to bring something to your attention.

In business, it is easy to assume that your vendors are looking out for you, always thinking about how to help you be better, more competitive, more strategic. But in my experience, that was rarely the case; this gave Red Apples Media the opportunity to distinguish itself by setting the standard that our own clients would then hold other vendors to.

I constantly challenged my team and myself to outthink our clients, staying a step ahead of them. When a client brought something to our attention that we were already aware of, researching, or working on, we took great pride in letting them know we were already on it.

When a new client joined the Red Apples Media portfolio, I pledged that it was more likely they would have to ask us to stop being so proactive with ideas and opportunities, rather than them calling us and saying, "How come I don't hear from you since I became a client?" So many companies have a great sales pitch on the front end and then the client becomes just another revenue stream once they've signed an agreement. That would not be the reputation of Red Apples Media.

Sometimes this would come in the form of seeing a strategically placed billboard, available for lease, with perfect placement for a client. Or, while scrolling through social media, noticing an upcoming community or professional event that aligns with a client's brand and target market.

In fact, I made it a goal to "groom" our own vendors—more specifically, media entities that were trying to gain a greater share of our clients' marketing budgets—to think proactively for us, so we could do so for our clients, making it beneficial for all.

Case in point: Red Apples Media would place sporadic cable-TV commercial campaigns for a local African American pastor to help market his multiple church locations. When he first came to us, he knew exactly where his audience was and when he wanted to reach them, laser focused on event programming on the cable channel Black Entertainment Television (BET). Specials like the National Association for the Advancement of Colored People's *NAACP Image Awards*, or the *BET Soul Train Awards*, were of great interest to him. While his church had some white congregants, the majority of those who attended were older Blacks.

As we talked more, and I learned more about his goals, we understood that—much like other organized religions across the country—the challenge of bringing in younger families, professionals, and singles was getting more difficult. We had to expand the target of our audience efforts.

In early 2020, I read about a new cable news start-up, Black News Channel (BNC). Its target viewer was a great supplement to the BET entertainment audience we were already reaching. I contacted my cable advertising rep, who not only didn't realize it had been added to our local system, she had not even heard of the channel. As such, we placed hundreds of commercials for "pennies a play" as an early ad adopter of the channel (they would file for bankruptcy two years later, but we leveraged it as long as we could).

As a result of us impressing the client with our forward thinking and knowledge of the marketplace, the pastor became more comfortable with approving opportunities that deviated from his original plan, assured that we would never lose sight of the broader goal of growing a more multigenerational congregation. It was also a valuable lesson for the cable sales rep, who became significantly better at proactively bringing opportunities to me, like a BET holiday movie marathon.

Similarly, in the summer of 2024, the Lake Mary baseball team was making an exciting run through the Little League World Series. These young men had become the darlings of central Florida. Not surprisingly, local cable ratings on ESPN were significantly higher than years past.

After a little digging, I confirmed the championship game would air that Sunday on the ABC stations. Lake Mary would still have to win a regional game and then the U.S. Championship game to make it to Sunday's World Series championship broadcast. I decided to roll the dice for our roofing client, who had four offices across central and northeast Florida, and called my local ABC station sales rep at about 1 p.m. on Friday:

Me: "I know it's late and you probably already have your weekend ads locked in, but do you have any open spots in Sunday's Little League World Series?"

Rep (after checking the ad sales logs): "I have two commercials available. And since we already have your client's commercial in our library, I can sneak them in if you let me know right away."

Me: "How much?"

Rep: "Can you do $100 each?"

By the way, earlier in my career, I worked in the advertising sales department at WFOR, the CBS TV station in Miami. Because of that experience, I always made sure the sales reps who worked with Red Apples Media knew that I understood the pressures of their job, while also making it clear that I knew how to play the ad sales game.

I had learned a great deal, including the steadfast rule, "Every rate is negotiable . . . usually." It's a game to determine who has the upper hand in ad sales negotiations. But because of my background, I was also sympathetic that they were trying to earn a living under the pressure of achieving sales goals set by higher-ups. I want to believe I was always reasonable and respectful, prioritizing the overall relationship, rather than nickel-and-diming every time we talked, while also looking out for our clients' best interests. A refreshing approach, I was often told.

In this case, I suspected my rep did not know why I was interested in advertising in that specific broadcast, and also recognized that those rates were an absolute steal (seriously, no pun intended). To even try to negotiate would likely have come back to haunt me down the road once he realized why I grabbed them—which I did.

Me: "Sold. Do me a favor and send me a text just to confirm you were able to get the order into the system, please."

Rep: "Consider it done. Have a great weekend."

My next call was to our client—one that we had already been working with for six years and had done a great deal to earn their trust in our judgment, integrity and stewardship of their advertising budget. It was rare that I would commit to something without the client's approval, but there was some isolated precedent.

Me: "Have you been following the Little League World Series?"

Client: "A little. There's a team from Florida playing really well, isn't there?"

Me: "There is. And the local hype has been growing as they get deeper into the tournament. So, here's what I did: I just bought two local commercials on our ABC station partner in the championship game on Sunday. They have to win two more games to get to the championship, but if they do, my bet is we will have record local TV ratings for the game."

Client: "How much?"

Me: "$200."

Client: "Each?"

Me: "For both."

Client: "That sounds really inexpensive, isn't it?"

Me: "I don't think the rep put it together when I called, so he was probably happy to put $200 on the books."

Client: "Good enough for me. Thanks for doing that."

Me: "And look, if they don't make it to the championship, I won't invoice you for the ads."

Client: "I assume, whether the Florida team is in it or not, people will still watch the game."

Me: "They always do. It's just that *more* people will watch around your service area if there is a local team playing."

Client: "Like I said, good enough for me."

P.S. The Lake Mary team *did* make it to the Little League World Series championship game, beating powerhouse Chinese Taipei, 2-1 in an incredible game.

After the game, I got a text from the rep:

"Sorry, forgot to text you on Friday. Spots ran. Great game."

And then:

"Well played. We're all going to have some explaining to do in Monday morning's sales meeting :)"

Your ability to grow a client and the services you provide them is typically more gratifying and more cost-effective than recruiting and onboarding a new client. Clients will rarely (OK, probably never) just let you keep spending their money without having earned the credibility of your commitment to them.

On the flip side of the previous examples, we had also made mistakes and proactively brought them to the client's attention, nearly always absorbing the cost of the error. It builds a great deal of trust and fortifies the strength of the relationship. It requires awareness and discipline to take a step back—exhibiting the integrity to acknowledge the error, learn from it, take whatever justifiable heat may come with it, and move forward. Few things are more gratifying than having an agency-client relationship tested over an error, only to have the client say, "Thank you for bringing it to my attention and covering the cost. I know it's not typical for your team to make an error like that. Moving on…"

Earlier in this chapter, I mentioned brown spots on my lawn. I use this as a frequent analogy in anticipating needs and opportunities (not to mention, accountability).

For a while, I had one company cutting my lawn, another checking the irrigation system, and a third provider treating the lawn with fertilizer and pest control. I was always the one to point out if there was something going on with the lawn that was of concern. None of my paid service providers ever knocked on my door and said, "Hey, you've got some brown spots that we need to look into and here's my plan."

Instead, the guy who cut the lawn would blame the irrigation guy, the irrigation guy would blame the treatment company, and the treatment company would criticize how poorly the lawn was being cut. Mind you, these are not inexpensive monthly services, and never did any of them take ownership or present a proactive approach to the problem.

Here's the thing, it really doesn't matter what business you're in. There will always be opportunities to organically and legitimately anticipate client needs and opportunities, then proactively present them to reinforce your understanding and appreciation of the relationship. Who doesn't want to be top of mind in a relationship?

There is an experiential difference between a restaurant server who comes up to your table and robotically asks, "Can I get you anything?" and the one who comes up to your table and notices that the water glasses need to be refilled, that the person who ordered the ribs has already burned through his original napkins and desperately needs more, and also brings the kid's menu with crayons to the toddler—a smart strategy, knowing the happier the toddler is, the longer and more enjoyable the meal will be.

There is also an experiential difference between the pool service company that simply swoops in, does the cursory cleaning, and moves to the next house, and the one that points out that the water is low, there's a bit of a drip and so they ordered a new gasket ("it's only five dollars, don't worry about it"), and tells you, "By the way, you're going to need a new filter in the next month or two—we can order it for you, or if you prefer to buy it yourself, just leave it out for us and we'll swap them."

This presents a challenging but invaluable opportunity for an organization to coach its people who do a fine job when they're on the clock, to adopt an entrepreneurial mindset when they're off the clock. I'm certainly not suggesting people need to think about work 24/7. However, I do believe that developing a heightened awareness of opportunities that may positively impact a client is a coachable skill.

It was a weekly requirement to bring new ideas, leads, competitive intel, and potential client opportunities to WFOR's weekly sales staff meeting. Similarly, the owner of another central Florida marketing agency shared with me that they have a standing requirement that every member of the staff, regardless of title or seniority, must provide two new business leads per quarter.

Successfully anticipating client needs and identifying beneficial opportunities are exponentially greater when the majority (if not all) of your team adopts an approach of open eyes, ears, and minds as a critical differentiator to serving customers at a higher level.

CHAPTER 9

INTERSTITIAL

Hey Big Boy!

It's difficult to have been employed for as long as I have, in as many capacities as I have, and not have experienced some extremely emotional, if not traumatic, days.

There was the day I found out from ownership at The Villages that I would be laying off half of my one-hundred-person staff, many of whom I'd recruited and relocated and had only been employed with me for a year or two. There were also the two occasions when I had to call my wife to let her know I had lost my job. Those were tough days, to be sure.

But, without hesitation, I will tell you the most difficult day(s) began on Friday, March 3, 2000, around 4 p.m., when my desk phone rang at WTVJ (NBC, Miami). On the other end was my audibly shaken vice president of news counterpart, Ramon Escobar.

Ramon: "I need you in the newsroom. Now."

Me: "Are you OK?"

Ramon: "No. We think *Sky 6* crashed."

To this day I can still visualize my path as I raced out of my office, following the steps I took several times each day between the creative services office and the NBC6 newsroom. I'm pretty sure I heard my admin ask me what was going on. I didn't know yet, so I didn't answer.

There was a quiet shock permeating the newsroom by the time I hit the threshold. Ramon was surrounded by his talented and loyal team, either stoic or with early tears. Ramon motioned for me to follow him and a couple of his managers into his office.

By then it was confirmed. The relatively new, state-of-the art news helicopter, *Sky 6*, had crashed to the ground near Kendall-Tamiami Executive Airport, killing the pilot and WTVJ photojournalist Rob Pierce.

Rob, a fellow graduate from the UF College of Journalism and Communications (he was a couple of years ahead of me), was extremely talented and passionate about news gathering, and took immense pride in the role he played in telling a story through his video camera lens.

In the newsroom was a shelf of TVs, each showing the competing stations' programming, 24/7, lest anyone break news and NBC6 not know about it. Within minutes of the accident, our competitor stations had all scrambled their own news choppers and broke into programming with aerial footage of *Sky 6* smoldering on the ground. Our tragedy had become the news, and it was a sickening feeling.

One thing I will tell you about the department head leadership team at WTVJ during my time, it was extremely cohesive. Much of this was driven by the militaristic approach of president and general manager, Don Browne, in how he managed "his lieutenants."

There was no time for emotions. Our own news coverage for the day was beginning in about an hour, and WTVJ would be the lead story across every newscast—including our own—eventually making national and even international news (I happened to be the department head "on call" when asked to do a phone interview with BBC Radio one evening).

I believe Don was out of town, elsewhere in Florida, at the time, but he had been called and was on his way back to the station. Ramon, always an impressive leader and someone I looked to for how to handle specific situations, took over. He divided people into news coverage, internal support, and message management. Another one of Don's favorite expressions was, "If you don't manage the message, the message will manage you."

There were so many questions, so many things to do, family to notify, a memorial to plan, and shock and grieving within the newsroom, all of which had to be strategically and simultaneously managed. It was truly all-hands-on-deck, no matter what department you worked in.

The department heads and many of the staff stayed at the station, waiting for Don to arrive. Once there, he immediately convened the newsroom leadership and various department managers. We debriefed him about what we knew, what steps we had taken, and what still needed to be done.

Over the next several days and throughout the weekend, department heads took shifts, so one or more of us was always at the station, around the clock. When we went home, it was to clean up, change clothes, and typically turn right back around, maybe with a quick nap and something to eat (other than the order-in meals at the office). If we weren't in the building for meetings, we would call from home into a toll-free conference call number several times throughout the day.

And that's when "it" happened, as I was dialing in from home, late that Saturday night. But it would have to wait until our next in-person meeting for me to share what I had accidentally done, for full effect.

That next morning, the core team arrived at the station for the first briefing of the day. Everyone was tired, filters were breaking down, and we were starting to see small cracks in our own armor, individually and as a group. Exhaustion and emotions can have that effect.

Don started with some small talk as we were settling in, asking how everyone was holding up. I felt like we needed something to lighten the mood, so I asked if I could share something I discovered by accident.

I reached for the large speaker phone in the middle of the conference room table. As I was dialing, I explained how I accidentally dialed an 800 version of the call-in number the night before, rather than the correct 888 version. With the phone on speaker, it rang three or four times until a sultry female recorded voice welcomed our call: "Hey, big boy. Thanks for calling. Are you ready for the hottest call of your life?"

I disconnected the call. That was really all we needed to hear. Lesson learned about paying closer attention to properly dialing phone numbers in the future.

I didn't get the roar of laughter I would have expected, but it was enough to break the tension and give everyone a much-needed smile. Plus, it also opened the door to my being greeted in the hallways by those around the table as, "Hey, big boy," for some time afterward.

With permission from Don, who agreed we all needed some personal time, I left the station on Sunday for a therapeutic afternoon of Florida spring training baseball with a close friend and his young son, who has always been like a nephew to me. As hard as I tried to clear my head and focus on the game and the company I was in, it was my first chance to absorb what had happened. It was the first time I allowed myself to feel grief, knowing that the armor would have to be back on as soon as I returned to the station the next morning.

There is a lot more to say about this experience, but it's neither my place, nor pertinent to this particular interstitial. I will add as a footnote, WTVJ established a scholarship endowment at the UF College of Journalism and Communications in Rob's memory. It was created to honor his legacy and passion for TV photojournalism, "to be awarded to students planning to pursue careers in television/electronic news videography; preference to students from Miami-Dade, Broward and Monroe counties."

I concluded this interstitial, debating whether to include the following anecdote or not. After long, thoughtful consideration, I decided it was a valuable and important residual from this horrific experience, which would come back to affect me many decades later.

As I mentioned earlier, Don Browne and I had a complicated relationship. I know I am not the only one who worked for Don over the years to use that adjective, but I'll stick to my own experiences, rather than invoking those of others.

As the president and general manager of a General Electric/NBC-owned television station, Don had a lot of responsibility and, I would assume, a great deal of pressure. He was hardheaded, competitive, driven, and, most times, direct and militaristic in how he managed people, particularly his VPs and other direct reports. He often used sports analogies and references to "coaching" to make his points and drive his "teams."

The Florida Marlins had just won the 1997 World Series, and Don—who many observed closely resembled Marlin's manager Jim Leyland—borrowed a Leyland uniform from the team and did a great impression during a station-wide "rally." Also a huge Miami Heat basketball fan, Don admired and drew from legendary Heat coach Pat Riley. In other words, while very influential on many careers (including mine, both good and bad), he was stoic and rarely let any emotion show other than anger.

Which is why—several days into the chopper crash events—I was so caught off guard when Don finally snapped. Oddly, it came as I felt things were starting to settle, plans were being finalized, some degree of normalcy was returning to the station, and we were doing our best to get back to the tasks at hand.

By this time, about a week or so after that horrific day, our department head meetings were now more of a casual check-in at the end of day. Don and Ramon had absorbed the brunt from a leadership perspective, and someone around the table asked Ramon how he was holding up. It was even suggested that perhaps he take a day or two off for himself. Before Ramon could respond, Don reacted in a way that I had not seen after almost two years of working for him.

"What about me? Nobody's asked about how I'm holding up. No one's suggesting I should take time off. I need to be supported, too, you know."

I can't tell you anything that happened after that. Did he continue? Did anyone respond? Did he storm out of the conference room?

All I know is that phrase, "*I need to be supported, too, you know,*" would forever be burned into my mental hard drive. Perhaps this was a subtle glimpse into some level of humanity and emotion from a man who prided himself on keeping it together and making sure those around him did the same.

Instead, I found myself wondering, "How could a guy who carried his title and significant financial compensation act so immaturely and selfishly? He was the leader and leaders don't crack. In fact, wasn't it *his* responsibility to make sure we were OK, and not the other way around?" I had neither the courage nor enough interest to follow the bear into the proverbial den to gain better understanding at that moment.

Frankly, I never understood his reaction—until I was running my own company.

There are times being an entrepreneur can be very lonely. You're constantly having to put on a brave face, and lead everyone to believe in you and that everything is going as planned. However, I learned over the years that there is a "firewall" when it comes to candor and transparency, particularly with staff. Exactly where that wall stood would shift depending on the circumstances, the staff, and the relationships. This is what I've referred to as "entrepreneurial solitude," and it can be both mentally and physically exhausting.

Over time, I would gain better understanding about what Don meant and why he reacted the way he did. We're all human and we all have our limitations and breaking points. It's easy for someone who is making twenty dollars an hour to look at the owner of a company and think, "You made the choice to start a business and all that goes with it, so I see no reason to be sympathetic to your challenges and emotions." They may not be malicious, but they would be wrong.

There is no shame in showing humanity, at any level of leadership. There is no shame in sharing a crack in the armor now and then. And there is no weakness in accepting genuine kindness and concern from those around you.

We *all* need to support, and we *all* need to be supported.

CHAPTER 10

People Are Our Priority. Relationships Drive Success.

I suck at sales. There, I said it. Always have, always will. Instead, give me an audience that I can engage with, whether a small group in a meeting room, one person over a cup of coffee, or in front of a large gathering at a fundraising event. Those kinds of scenarios give me a much better chance to create a relationship. In some cases, those relationships span several years, with the average longevity of a Red Apples Media client lasting around seven years. Other times, that relationship connection only requires a few critical hours, such as emceeing an event to help raise funds for an impactful organization.

Throughout my years in television, it was often suggested I should move from creative services to sales, especially if I wanted to climb the corporate ladder and "really make some money." I resisted every offer, determined not to become a salesperson as I defined one in my mind. This was actually rather ironic, since the majority of my TV career was in promotions, where my teams and I were responsible for driving viewership for the various stations I worked at. It occurred to me later on that, in fact, I was in sales—the station was my client, and the viewers were the consumers. I was selling the station, its newscasts and other programming, to gain the largest share of audience we could.

The first time I went for a haircut during my stint in Bangor, the young lady cutting my hair asked me what I did for a living. Fresh out of college and feeling rather proud of my title at WABI, I replied that I was the director of promotions at Channel 5. She stopped cutting, looked at me over my shoulder in the mirror with an expression that indicated she was duly impressed.

"Wow. You must be really popular at work."

I looked at her, confused, and asked what she meant.

"Well, aren't you the one who decides who gets a promotion?" But I digress.

It's not uncommon when you're starting up a business to focus on short-term cash flow—trying to do anything you can to make a sale and get the funds rolling in—while also working to establish credibility with new clients by already having a roster of existing ones. I had made several tactical errors during the first few months of introducing the innovative, but unknown, concept of Hometown Health TV (HHTV) to medical practitioners.

Since HHTV was unique in that it was specialty exclusive (we would only have, for example, one podiatrist in the network during the length of the contract), I would sometimes casually mention how I was also scheduled to meet with a direct competitor. I wasn't. Or, I would increase the rate so I could offer a discount. I never felt right about any of this, but these were some of the "tricks" I had learned from working with some (not all) TV salespeople, designed to create demand and expedite decisions.

On one occasion, I sold a subscription to a physician who I knew in my gut would not benefit from the investment, and would, in all likelihood, have an adverse impact on the overall monthly episode. I'm not sure where he was from, but he had a very heavy foreign accent, which made it difficult to understand him. Compound that with the fact that he was dry, monotone, and did not know how to communicate his exceptional medical knowledge to a layperson television audience. He wanted in, we needed the income, so we signed him up.

After just a few episodes, I knew I was spot-on with my concerns, both for him and the HHTV program. Each sixty-minute episode—which would feature a two-to-three-minute segment about each contracted specialist—would come to a grinding halt when his segment came on. He began to express concern about his investment and told me four months before the end of his twelve-month agreement that he would not be renewing. I apologized for his disappointment and let him out of the contract early, hoping to salvage the relationship, and the potential of doing some ancillary marketing work for the practice.

That experience was an epiphany for me. I realized that I needed to focus more on building long-term relationships, with less worry on "diving for dollars." I made a conscious decision to focus on quality, value, and "delivering on commitments while overdelivering on expectations."

Shortly after that, I went to a business lunch with another potential practitioner and his fiancée—who also served as their office manager. I left the pitch book back at my office and instead we just had a casual conversation over lunch, during which I explained what HHTV was and how I believed it would benefit their chiropractic practice. I put a lot of emphasis on value but never discussed pricing and never made an ask. Typically, the lack of an ask would be mocked by a "true salesperson." But I was feeling much better about this approach than any I had tried previously.

Late in the lunch, doc's fiancée smiled at me and said, "You've read the book, haven't you?" I honestly thought she was referring to the Bible, but I needed to be careful.

Me: "I'm not sure what book you're referring to."

Her: "*The Go-Giver.*"

Me: "The go-getter?"

Her: "No, *The Go-Giver*. You talk and use phrases as if you've already read it."

Me: "Not familiar, but it sounds like something I should check out."

Now, I could have left lunch and simply headed back to the office, or I could have recognized a sign from The Universe (patience, only a few chapters more). I drove to the only major bookstore in the area and purchased a copy of *The Go-Giver* by Bob Burg and John David Mann.[4]

The chiropractic office did not sign on as an HHTV client, but more importantly, the book recommendation would become profoundly influential for me, both personally and professionally. It changed how I approached and prioritized people. It took me out of a sales mindset and put me into one of building relationships, particularly ones in which I had no expectation of immediate gain. I know a lot of people say they're all about relationships. I was determined to live it.

The specific use of the phrase within this core value, "Relationships Drive Success," intentionally does not suggest monetary gain, although that could be a residual. If your focus is money, you'll often wind up with a one-sided reward. When you approach building value into a relationship and sharing that value and relationship with others, success (as you define it) will become self-fulfilling and more gratifying.

I'm reminded of one client in particular who became a friend outside of the client relationship. He would bust my chops about always asking five questions. No matter the topic—and whether via email, text, phone call, or in person—he caught on that I asked a lot of questions, and observed that five tended to be my magic number. He was right.

This characteristic comes from a few places. First and foremost, I'm a naturally inquisitive person, likely one of the reasons I started down the road of journalism in college (pivoting to creative at some point, but still in TV and media). More important, I believe people inherently like talking about themselves, sharing their knowledge and stories, even if they tell you they don't like to talk about themselves. You just have to know how to ask the right questions the right way. Equally important, you need to know how to listen the right way.

The more we know about someone, the easier it is to find common ground to serve as the foundation for the relationship. I think you will also find that people will start to open up more easily as they get more comfortable, and recognize that your interest is genuine and your respect for confidentiality is unwavering. To this day, I am stunned by the things clients have shared with me in confidence—often before telling staff, business partners, and sometimes even spouses—all out of a deep, humbling level of earned loyalty and trust.

When you break it down, don't we all want those kinds of relationships?

It would be inauthentic of me to not also bring up where I have fallen short in this core value—with my own people.

I initially introduced the RED APPLES core values by producing mouse pads for all the office workstations with a graphic depiction of the nine core values. I also printed and framed posters, hanging them on the walls throughout the office. Shortly after the introduction, someone I had hired to serve as Red Apples Media's operations manager called me out during a difficult but impactful private conversation.

"How can people be your priority, but you don't prioritize the needs of your own people?"

Slap!

Of course, my first instinct was to go on the defensive, but I had known Jenn for quite some time prior to bringing her on board and had a great deal of respect for her perspective, not to mention her courage to hold me accountable.

One of the reasons I had hired an ops manager was because I was growing frustrated with my team and I needed an intermediary. Among other things, I wrestled greatly with my failure to understand why everyone at Red Apples Media didn't have an entrepreneurial mindset and treat the company as if it was their own. For example, I have always made monetary commission on new business available to anyone at Red Apples, no matter their title. Unfortunately, most took the position of, "I'm not a salesperson," and refused to even entertain the possibility of taking advantage of this lucrative option.

In an effort to creatively address this, I decided to freeze everyone's hourly increases, and tied them instead to a company performance bonus structure. My hope was that by giving them a financial interest in the success of the company, they would be more engaged and take greater ownership of not only their own work and efforts, but that of the company as a whole.

It was clear that they would earn more money with this structure than through the traditional 3-to-5 percent annual pay increase. However, there was no guarantee of a bonus, and no indication of amount, or frequency, until it was calculated (although I had committed to quarterly evaluations). Typically, the greatest bonuses would come at the end of the year, once I had a confident feel for how the company's financials would shake out in December. For perspective, my approach to paying myself as the owner of Red Apples Media was to wait until the end of the month, make sure everyone and everything else was paid, and then determine an appropriate amount to pay myself, which could range dramatically from month to month.

Drawing from two years of the bonus structure, I was able to clearly show that the financial benefit was closer to 12-to-15 percent, annually. A no-brainer, in my mind.

But Jenn made some very valuable observations, arguing that the staff shared with her that the bonus approach created a great deal of stress for them. The unpredictability of not knowing from quarter to quarter and year to year what their compensation would be was not worth the undisputed financial upside. Their concerns were driven by their individual inability to reliably budget for certain expenses, plan for vacations, pay off bills, etc.

"Welcome to my world," I thought.

It was also a time when I was feeling a lack of appreciation for anything I felt I was doing to make Red Apples a great place to work. Surprise field trips away from the office, a "thank-you" gift card or spot bonus for a particular job well done on a project, or even the occasional "Anyone up for pizza for lunch today, my treat?" often all going without any recognition or appreciation.

When we get to the *L* core value, you'll also gain a better understanding of how I tried to incorporate community projects into the office. For example, every year I would put out a big box in the lobby for a two-week school supply drive. I could never get the staff to add supplies to the box. Whenever we were sponsoring an event or a volunteer opportunity that might include some evening or weekend hours, it was always followed by, "Are we getting paid?"

This was both foreign and maddening to me. So, I just stopped trying.

Jenn pointed out that, in fact, they were all very philanthropic with either their time or money. It's just that it was on their time, on their terms, based on their own passions, and not necessarily in alignment with what was important to me and the projects that aligned with the Red Apples brand and our reputation in the community.

What I learned was that it was equally important, if not more so, to know that I had hired people who did share my values, even if they didn't share my vision of how and when to express them.

We had done a great job of prioritizing the people who were clients and business partners. But this powerful conversation with Jenn forced me to recognize that I had to recalibrate how I applied this core value to my own team, leading me to reinstitute hourly pay rate adjustments (still with modest bonus opportunities) and create a program in which Red Apples Media would match dollars donated to local nonprofits by staff.

A few short years later, Red Apples Media would be named a "2024 Best Place to Work" by the local newspaper publisher.

CHAPTER 11

INTERSTITIAL

The Duke Of York Road

I am very aware and grateful that my career path has included a great number of personal celebrity interactions. For the most part, I would say they were all very positive, some more than others. It would be extremely rare that I would—in the course of my job—host a television or sports celebrity who was not, at the very least, cordial. Most were genuinely fun, down-to-earth, and appreciative of my efforts and hospitality.

On January 1, 1995, WMAR-TV (Baltimore) was part of an unprecedented three-way station affiliation switch. Meaning, WMAR switched from NBC to ABC, WBAL switched from CBS to NBC, and WJZ switched from ABC to CBS. You can research why all of this happened on your own, but as the creative services director at WMAR, it was an extraordinary six months, preparing for the New Year's Day "flip of the switch."

Throughout this period, we relied on "star power" to help guide viewers and reorient them to turn to our station for their favorite ABC programming. Our strategy was an educational approach, so, along with local ad agency WB Doner, we enlisted actor and economist Ben

69

Stein—perhaps best known as the monotone teacher in the eighties film *Ferris Bueller's Day Off.*

We worked with Ben on set for two days, creating a series of promotional commercials, one of which also included Maryland's own Pat Sajak, from *Wheel of Fortune.*

Ben Stein and Maryland's Pat Sajak on-set together during the WMAR-TV affiliation switch promotional production

Ben was one of the sweetest, kindest people I had ever met, celebrity or otherwise. He was easy to work with, never complained, had great stories to tell, and never missed a chance to graze the snack and meal table. At one point, he pulled me aside and mentioned that he noticed that I never ate while we were working. I explained that I didn't have time. While he was resting, we were resetting for the next shot or tweaking the scripts.

At the end of the production, I asked Ben to sign the 8x10 photo of us that I had printed at the local photo store. Ben punctuated his point with what he wrote: "To Marc, who never has any time for lunch. I do. Your friend, Ben Stein."

Ben Stein and me on set with his not-so-subtle reminder
about the importance of breaking for lunch

In the summer of 1995, we partnered with a Maryland theme park and hosted daytime television celebrities for a local version of the "ABC Super Soap Weekend." Our slate included John York and Vanessa Marcil, both from the *General Hospital* cast, as well as a young Nathan Fillion, who was on ABC's *One Life to Live*. There is a lot to share about this experience, but for the sake of space, let me tell you about John York.

My mementos from hosting John, Vanessa, and Nathan
during the ABC Super Soap Weekend

John was flying into Baltimore from Los Angeles, arriving early evening. I had been in touch with his publicist the entire time, who had made it very clear that John would be tired from the long flight and working all week. She made a point of letting me know he would want to go directly to the hotel. I was also told not to draw attention to his arrival by holding a sign with his name. I assumed this was so he could get through the airport without being disturbed by fans. I couldn't help but wonder if this was going to be a high maintenance weekend.

I rode in the limousine to personally greet him at the airport. Remember, this was pre-9/11, so I was able to meet him at the gate and knew he would be among the first to get off the plane from first class. Not a viewer of "*GH*," I recognized him from his publicity photo and introduced myself. I had prepared for a cranky celebrity, but instead what I got was a huge smile, firm handshake/hug, and his "Thanks for having me. I'm really looking forward to this." He had already knocked me off my game, quickly defying all the assumptions I made about him based on my interactions with his publicist.

He got a few head turns as we walked to the car, but he was more interested in me, what I did for the station, how long I had been in television, how I liked Baltimore, etc. Once in the car, he asked me where we were headed. I explained that his publicist instructed me to take him to the hotel. John had his own plan. Noting that it was dinnertime and correctly assuming that I had not eaten yet, he suggested we should go to dinner.

I offered a high-end steakhouse that was a frequent "go-to" for special occasions and out-of-town guests. He wanted to know if there was a college campus nearby with a restaurant near campus that I liked.

Bill Bateman's Bistro, one of my favorites, was adjacent to the Towson University campus. To further support my recommendation, I pointed out the irony that Bateman's was located on (wait for it) York Road. John York decided that it was serendipitous, and we were off.

His motives still had not clicked for me, but this is what my guest wanted to do, and I was his host.

I can't imagine many limos ever pulled up to Bateman's, so our black stretch triggered some understandable curiosity. As we walked in, it only took moments before I started to notice John was drawing attention. The hostess, a college-aged female, must have known who he was and asked if we wanted to sit somewhere private, but John wanted to be on the outside patio.

We sat, John looked at me and said, "We're doing this weekend for the fans, right? Why not start now? Get ready."

I swear we had only been sitting for maybe two minutes before the first female college-aged student mustered the courage to approach the table.

"Excuse me, are you Mac Scorpio from *GH*?"

John replied, "I am. John York, and this is my friend Marc. Very nice to meet you."

For perspective, this was all before smartphones, and basic cell phones were just coming to market. Looking back, I can't fathom how so many college girls found out John York was at Bateman's as quickly as they did. As the night progressed, they started showing up with film cameras and items to autograph. Those who were not in the restaurant as patrons lined the railing of the outside patio. They were all very polite, but also very eager to get John's attention.

He introduced his "friend Marc" to everyone who came over to the table, only to have them be disappointed when they realized I was not a celebrity. He signed autographs, answered questions, posed for pictures, and loved every minute of it. I was awed by his patience, charm, and genuine appreciation for the attention. He knew these young, female college students were an important part of his core audience and without them, his longevity on *GH* would undoubtedly be shortened.

In other words, he prioritized the people and those brief relationships with each and every fan, understanding the role the viewers (through ratings) played in his success and that of *General Hospital*.

We did finally get to eat and then it was time for me to get John to his hotel, so I could ride back to the airport to pick up Vanessa and Nathan—who were dating at the time and coming in on a later flight.

Candidly, I was immediately captivated by Vanessa's beauty, but also by how laid back and immediately funny, if not punchy from the flight, Nathan was. In fairness, my then-girlfriend Nanci (now my wife)—who joined us at the weekend event at John's suggestion the night before—was equally captivated by Nathan, and she would have no problem admitting it, even to this day.

Nathan and John, who did not know each other very well, hit it off like a couple of college buddies. They provided endless entertainment both behind the scenes and in public over the course of their short visit to represent ABC daytime soaps for the Maryland fans. I'm not sure if Vanessa felt left out or perhaps resented having to share Nathan's attention with John, but she was clearly not enjoying the assignment the way the boys were.

Hanging out with the soap stars was the second time Nanci had a brush with my celebrity guests visiting Baltimore.

Prior to the "ABC Super Soap Weekend," WMAR held a huge advertiser party to celebrate the affiliation switch from NBC to ABC. We had another group of celebrities come in for that event as well, including the late Alex Trebek (WMAR was the on-air home to both *Wheel of Fortune* and *Jeopardy*).

Nanci and I had gone to dinner in downtown Baltimore the same night the celebrity guests were coming to town and checking into a nearby hotel overlooking Baltimore's Inner Harbor. After dinner, I suggested we stop by the hotel and see if anyone had checked in yet. I would know by how many of the welcome baskets—which I had left at the front desk earlier in the day—were already gone.

Alex Trebek's limo pulled up to the hotel just as we walked up. I held the front door for him as he walked in, trying to introduce myself and thanking him for traveling for the station's event. Trebek never broke stride, never turned around, and headed right for the front desk. I followed him, explaining there was a gift basket waiting for him that also included everything he would need to know for the next night, including what time the car would pick him and the other celebrities up to take them to the venue. The information sheet also included my home and mobile number, in case anyone needed anything.

I wished him a good night, Nanci and I left the hotel, and we drove back to our apartment. I couldn't help but be a bit disappointed in our initial interaction with Trebek.

The next afternoon, I was at the venue setting up when my mobile phone rang. It was Nanci, almost giddy.

Nanci: "Guess who I just talked to."

Me: "No idea."

Nanci: "Alex Trebek called the apartment."

Me: "You're kidding. What did he say?"

Nanci: "He wanted to know what time he was getting picked up and how he was getting to the event." (All of which was included on the information sheet in the basket I tried to tell him about.)

Me: "Did he phrase it in the form of a question?"

This is one of our favorite stories and our only regret was that the answering machine didn't pick up to record his message.

A final footnote on Vanessa. I ran into her again at another publicity event about three years later. By then she had become a more mainstream actress, appearing in the movie *The Rock* and now promoting her new NBC show, *Las Vegas*.

Me: "You probably don't remember, but we met a few years ago."

Vanessa: "Do you work on the third floor?"

Me: "No. I hosted you, Nathan, and John York in Baltimore for the 'Super Soap Weekend' event, a few years ago."

Vanessa: "I remember!" *Short pause.* "That was a horrible trip!"

She affirmed what I had thought she was feeling back in Baltimore, but I didn't care. The event was a success, the guys had a blast—and she still looked spectacular.

CHAPTER 12

Profits Are A Function Of Integrity, Not Sales

This core value goes hand-in-hand with the previous one.

It was an opportunity for me to pull a few of the previous values together and reiterate the importance of integrity, relationships, and the idea that clients, sales, and revenue would be a residual—not a driver—of my very specific approach to building Red Apples Media. Again, this is a summation on my part of some of the primary takeaways from *The Go-Giver* book.

This concept can be argued, and it has been (more on that in a minute). It breaks nearly every sales training strategy that focuses on the *quantity* of attempts and the notion that it is "a numbers game"—the more calls, the better the chances for positive outcomes. Instead, Red Apples Media chose to focus on *quality* client relationships, building its reputation as a company that operated with the highest level of integrity, a great deal of transparency, and proactive accountability.

Right around the time our Florida home turned thirteen years old, I started to worry a little about our roof. Other homes of similar age in our neighborhood were starting to get reroofed, casualties of the punishing summer storms, a couple of Category 1 hurricanes and outer bands, and the blazing year-round sun and heat. My concern grew as I noticed more and more shingle granules in my rain gutters.

I first turned to our next-door neighbor, whose home—a couple of years older than ours—already had its roof redone a few months earlier. Trusting their vetting process (not to mention, they literally knew everyone in the community, and everyone knew them), I contacted their roofer and dropped our neighbor's name as the referral source.

Brian from Covenant Roofing came to our home the next evening after I got home from work. He spent about thirty minutes on our roof and came down with about three dozen photos on his tablet and walked me through what he saw. The bottom line was that he agreed the roof was showing age, but he felt it had at least another year or two before we really needed to be concerned. Read that line again: A roofer who could have told me anything, chose integrity by letting me know he didn't need to sell us anything at that moment in time. I was blown away.

A little skeptical, I called another well-known roofing company in our community and asked for an estimate. A few mornings later, I left through my front door (I typically come and go through the garage) and noticed a piece of paper sticking out from under our door mat. It was a 5x7 sheet from one of those carbon pads with a handwritten estimate. I never knew anyone from the company had come to our house and I had no idea how they had arrived at the estimate, let alone whether they even inspected the roof.

About a year and a half later, I had an unrelated need for someone to be on our roof. When the service technician came down, he mentioned that I may want to have a roofer check it out since it was showing some wear and aging.

It was time to give Covenant Roofing another call. "Hey Brian, remember me from about a year ago?"

Brian came back, updated his photos, sat with me and my wife, and went through an extensive presentation. He reviewed the timeline, costs, and even the variables that would not be known until the old roof was removed. It was going to cost more than I thought, but he had already won my trust and there was value in our time.

As we were sitting and filling out paperwork, he noticed the Red Apples Media logo on my shirt and asked what I did for a living. After I explained, he indicated they were in growth mode and had been talking about needing a marketing company that could grow with them. He stated that they were trying to change the customer perception of the roofing industry, which I had already experienced firsthand. This was exactly the kind of character and challenge we were looking for in the clients we were adding to our strategically growing roster. *Ah, The Universe* (keep reading, you're getting closer to that chapter).

Covenant Roofing would become one of Red Apples Media's largest clients as we joined them on an extraordinary journey from one office serving central Florida to four offices serving nearly all the state.

Along the way, this faith-based, family-owned company, worked with our team, adopting and trademarking the spiritually inspired slogan, "The Difference Is the Promise."

To this day, I find myself using them as an example of Red Apples's success and the importance of working with clients who shared our commitment to integrity.

In contrast, we also had a high-profile client who was arrested twice—once for allegedly scheming a murder-for-hire to eliminate one of his competitors and the second time for alleged drunk and disorderly conduct during an overseas flight. Both made the local news. We parted ways, despite our revenue loss.

Over the years, I tried many times to hire "salespeople." During one memorable interview, I was meeting with a woman who came from a traditional media sales background. As we sat in our conference room with the RED APPLES core values framed and hanging on the wall, she began to ask how we were currently gaining new business. I explained that, by that time, it was almost entirely from word of mouth and referrals. However, I felt that a person who was focused full-time on bringing in new business would be an asset to growing our company and client base.

I listened as she told me about all her tactics, strategies, and what a great closer she had been at her previous sales jobs. She went on to brag about her ability to even get previous clients to sign on for services she wasn't even sure the company was capable of, but "money is money," and that was a significant reason for her financial success as a salesperson.

I should have politely wound down the interview, thanked her for her time, and sent the "good luck in your search" email the next day. But I did not. I followed her pitch by explaining that we were not particularly interested in strategies and closing tactics. Our success came from bringing on clients that we knew we were completely capable of delivering (or overdelivering) what we promised, driven by being held accountable. Focused on growing and evolving relationships with clients we respected and liked working with, I pointed to the core values on the wall and drew her attention to the second *P*.

I will never forget the next thing she said, word for word: "Well, I disagree with that statement, and I think it's naive."

"Perhaps," I replied. "But it works for us."

Maybe that was not one of her best closing strategies.

Over time it became increasingly important to know when to turn work and clients away. That too may be counterintuitive, but it also becomes a bit of a luxury as you grow, become more stable as a business, and develop a brand based on an elevated level of integrity that others hold you to.

Sometimes we would refer an opportunity to another provider that we thought could better handle the needs. Sometimes it was a smaller agency or solo entrepreneur that had more flexibility with smaller budgets. Sometimes the client's need did not align with our skill set. For example, when it came to video production, I often explained, "We don't do weddings and bar mitzvahs. That is a specific skill set, and there are people better suited for that work."

On occasion we would get pushback, either because they really wanted to work with us, or they didn't understand why any company would turn away new business. A couple of times, the contact even got a little belligerent about our decision to respectfully decline the work. I should point out, being belligerent never made me change my mind about turning down business. Instead, such tone and behavior just reinforced that we were making the right decision.

After all, we believed it was more important that we stayed true to our brand and values as part of a long-term strategy of integrity driving profit. We understood and acknowledged this might come at the risk of lost sales or revenue.

But, hey:

"If you don't stick to your values when they're being tested, they're not values, they're hobbies," said the sage talk show host Jon Stewart.[5]

CHAPTER 13

INTERSTITIAL

Golden Brain

Typically, humans inherently tend to favor one side of their brain over the other. The left side is usually associated with logic and analytics, while the right side drives a person's creativity. Those who tend to be balanced in their ability to utilize both hemispheres of their brain are referred to as having a "golden brain."

I'm not aware of any study that has researched the rarity, if any, of such people, but I do know firsthand that right-side dominant, creative people tend to struggle with the left side's analytical functions. Case in point, several very creative people have left Red Apples Media over the years with the idea of starting their own creative company of some kind. To the best of my knowledge, nearly all gave up their entrepreneurial efforts—not because they are not creative and talented, but because they struggle with the business side of owning a business.

I cannot begin to tell you how many freelancers I have hired over the years that I had to badger to get invoices for their work. After all, what's the point in working if you're not going to get paid for it? I'm not judging, but it is a cautionary tale that demands consideration of a very important factor when deciding whether you are suited to be a creative entrepreneur, particularly one who is responsible for the livelihood of others.

I always felt very blessed and confident in my creative, right-side talents and abilities.

But having been given managerial responsibilities very early in my career, I had to learn budgeting, forecasting, and analytics. These were all critical in my ability to develop and grow Red Apples Media, not to mention managing budgets for clients and employers, sometimes in the seven- and eight-figure realms.

The annual budget process at some of my jobs was typically a grind. We were very often asked to look into a crystal ball and make an educated guess about expenses and revenue in the coming year, which may not even begin for another four to six months. At the time part of the subsidiary of General Electric's owned group of NBC stations, WTVJ had a responsibility for being profitable for its shareholders. Each year we were tasked with achieving a hard return on investment (ROI) number, which would drive our budget projections.

It was not uncommon for the department heads to come together toward the end of the process, usually on a weekend, and lock horns over defending their needs as we whittled down the final numbers to hit the desired ROI. During one such meeting, we were still several hundreds of thousands of dollars over budget and looking at everything from postage to head count to close the gap.

If you've ever owned a business or managed a marketing budget, you know how easy and common it is for businesses to turn to marketing as a budget line for savings, seeing marketing as a cost rather than an investment. As the vice president of creative services, I was responsible for the internal and external marketing and promotion of WTVJ. No surprise then that I was particularly dug in, defending my department, people, and our budgetary needs to meet the ratings goals, which we were also projecting to drive the revenue side of the budget (higher ratings meant the station could charge advertisers higher rates for airing commercials on the station).

We were getting tired, animated, and chippy. Ramon Escobar, the vice president of news, used to refer to these as "dynamic, spirited debates" (I still use that phrase). But we were still being pushed to think creatively and strategically.

Maybe it was exhaustion, youthful stupidity, or brazen courage, but I pointed out that one news anchor's salary represented the entire amount we were looking to trim. I wondered out loud, "Wouldn't it be less painful for one person to go home and tell their family that their six-figure contract would not be renewed, than for as many as five or six people who cumulatively represented the same dollar amount?"

Cue the record scratch sound effect.

After being berated for the next few minutes about how the loss of such a prestigious anchor could set the station back for decades, I realized we weren't really looking for creative solutions, as unfathomable as my idea may or may not have been. So much for "thinking outside the box." In fact, this was one of the instances that led me to proudly coin one of my many "Marcisms" (definitely not to be confused with Marxism).

Thinking outside the box suggests at least one side of the box needs to be completely open. The idea is an unencumbered, free flow of ideas with no restrictions. I've wasted more time than I can imagine over the years participating in "torrential downpour brainstorming" sessions, when in fact, I prefer to encourage my team to "think inside the balloon." In other words,

---

We must acknowledge that we have restrictions—time, budget, resources, to name a few. By thinking inside the balloon, we take these restrictions into consideration and then work to stretch the balloon as far as we can before it pops.

I have found this to not only be more productive, but it also requires a level of professional discipline by all those participating, forcing them to focus on the task or challenge at hand, rather than pie-in-the-sky, never-gonna-happen ideas.

Think back to the scene in the film *Apollo 13* where NASA must figure out how to reduce the CO_2 in the capsule. Rather than wasting time, brainstorming ideas that would never achieve the result of saving lives in time, they worked with what they had on board the capsule (the balloon) and stretched the use of those items in ways never imagined or anticipated.[6]

COVID-19 was also an incredible test of businesses in general, particularly small ones. Following state-mandated orders from Florida's governor, the Red Apples Media team went remote for about seven weeks. Being in the video production business, not being able to go on location and interact with people, is like being in the T-shirt business without access to cotton.

We had to pivot, as I made a commitment to my team that I would do everything I could to make sure they did not lose any pay during this period. My only challenge to them was whether they were willing to adapt with me. Extensive experience in managing budgets, particularly expenses, helped us get through. Additionally, as more live events were turning to streaming and remote productions, we were able to leverage an earlier investment into video streaming equipment that no one else in the market was positioned to do.

All told, while I took a 30 percent pay cut for six months "out of an abundance of caution" (a phrase that still triggers COVID-period flashbacks for me) to keep extra cash on hand if needed, everyone kept their job and maintained nearly all their hours. When the restrictions were lifted and it was time to return to the office, all but one came back. She had been bit by the work-from-home bug and opted to start her own venture when I balked at her continuing to work remotely.

We had survived the test of COVID-19 on our business, and arguably made ourselves more valuable by expanding into service areas we had not previously considered. This enabled us to bring on new clients who did not need our traditional services but needed our adapted ones.

In all candor, having a "golden brain" can also be a burden at times. While I take great pride in my cerebral balance and abilities, I much prefer being creative. However, taking on the responsibility of owning a business, and being committed to your staff's ability to earn a living, demands a large degree of selflessness and awareness. If my role is better served as the driver of business and client development than jumping at a project that's more creative, I have a responsibility to go where the need is.

This is something for you budding creative entrepreneurs to strongly consider.

CHAPTER 14

Live For What You Love.
Work To Make A Difference.

aunching a business—even starting a new job—is demanding, if you're truly committed to it. As I mentioned, while highly compensated, my final few months at The Villages were emotionally and spiritually draining. It felt too often that all I was doing was collecting a paycheck with little gratification (or appreciation from the company) to show for it. Plus, anything that resembled a work-life balance was nonexistent. After leaving The Villages, I swore I would never let that happen again, no matter how hard I had to work to successfully get this new company off the ground in order to regain balance in my life, along with passion in my career.

There was one more consideration. By the time I was laid off in 2008, my daughter was now seven years old and very cognizant that something significant had happened, even if she did not fully understand. It was important to my wife and I that we use this opportunity to make sure our daughter learned through our actions the importance of contributing and making a difference in our community, while at the same time doing everything we could to minimize the impact that my lack of immediate income would have on her routine. In other words: Live for what you love. Work to make a difference.

This RED APPLES core value challenges you to define what or who you truly love, and what role that love plays in your life. You must also define what success looks like in determining how important is it for you to make a difference in your community (however you define your "community").

Structuring and incorporating this value was, in part, influenced by experiences from my youth.

As a kid, I grew up in a family business. My parents owned pharmacy/gift shops in New Jersey where my dad was the pharmacist, and my mom was the creative presence of the "front end" of the store. I'm oversimplifying what they did, and I won't get into the impact and family dynamics; however, I do have a point here, which is not intended to evolve into a counseling session.

My dad agreed to be the coach of my community league baseball team when I was eleven years old. His best friend (I called him "Doc" and he was also my godparent) agreed to share the coaching responsibilities with my dad, even though he did not have a son of his own on the team. I suspect my dad recruited his willing friend, knowing he was going to work some evenings, preventing him from attending games and even some practices. On the other hand, Doc was a partner in his established dental practice, enjoying more traditional medical office hours and having more control over his schedule. This way, he could be there when my dad could not. The team was at its best when both dad and Doc were in the dugout.

I recently had my mom send me a photo of that baseball team. It was the year we lost only one game (two, if you count the crushing 1-0 loss in the championship game). Missing from that team photo was my dad. He had to work the night the photo was taken. He also missed the night I got the call to be the starting pitcher, completing the game for the win. By no means is this intended to fault him or suggest that he put work before his family. It was a different time with different social norms, which included him working hard to provide for his family. On top of that, he was launching a business of his own while holding down a full-time job working as a pharmacist for someone else.

Our baseball team photo, taken on a night my dad had to work
(Doc is on the right—no recollection who the gentleman is on the left)

It would take decades, age, and maturity for this all to resonate with me and influence how I wanted to prioritize my life. This included recognizing how rare it is that working and living are fully independent of each other. For that reason, I often point out the order of the phrase, "work-life balance." It strongly suggests that working provides us with the means to enjoy life and care for those we love.

During the twenty years following college graduation, I moved (a lot), I advanced in my career, I married, and then I became a father.

Our daughter was born about a year before I started working at The Villages. As she grew older and was more aware of the home environment, it became more important to me to "live for what I loved" than to be as driven in my career as I had been leading up to her birth.

Remember, my wife had taken a buyout package from her employer six months before I got laid off. Her decision was partially driven by her desire to be more available for our daughter—more involved at her school, dance, Girl Scouts, swimming, or even the religious school my wife started at our local synagogue.

Yes, I put in long hours at the office getting Hometown Health off the ground, and consistently afterwards, as it grew into Red Apples Media. But if I had to pick "The Kid" up from somewhere, or she had an event of some kind, she probably never gave it a second thought whether I would be there. It was something I was committed to, and I was determined to deliver on that commitment. So much so, that it clearly had an impact on her, recollecting what she said a few years later (and I mentioned earlier in the *D* chapter) to the kind woman at the Incubator Business of the Year awards luncheon.

Technology and communication also proved to be a minefield in managing that balance. It's difficult to be present with the ones you love when your phone is constantly alerting you to emails and text messages, particularly during nights, weekends, and vacations. My clients learned very early on that I did not receive emails to my office address on my phone—by choice. While many had my cell number, they knew there had to be a significant reason to text me outside of office hours, or risk my decision to reply "on my time, not thy time." Some were better at respecting this than others. Over time, I learned how to manage text conversations to respectfully and professionally discourage the texter's interruption of my personal time.

This strategic but deliberately disconnected approach confounded many of those who chose the 24/7 barrage of communication as their normal. At the same time, after getting over any perceived inconvenience of respecting my boundaries, they would all confess jealousy and admiration. Many, if not all, admitted they had already created too high of an expectation of technology-driven availability to reverse course in creating their own communication boundaries. I disagreed.

In turn, I was also very mindful to not text or call my staff when they were away from the office, unless it was also a time-sensitive or critical situation. In doing so, we established a high level of credibility that on the rare occasion they would hear from me or a coworker during their time *living for what they loved* (always beginning with an apology), there was significant importance behind the intrusion.

There are also many examples of how the two elements of this core value collide with each other, creating a sweet synchronicity.

Spending a lot of time with medical providers through Hometown Health, I also became more aware of wellness, diet, balancing stress, managing weight, staying active, and taking a proactive approach to my healthcare. So, when I turned fifty years old, I used my first colonoscopy to raise awareness in our community for the importance of preventative care. That effort would wind up not only in an episode of *Hometown Health*, but also in the local newspaper and the hospital's monthly newsletter, and it also resulted in one of Red Apples Media's many Telly Awards.

Similarly, as the main anchor of *Hometown Health*, I developed a humbling degree of local, small-town celebrity and a platform to feature our community. I was often asked to emcee or host events, fundraisers, presentations, and other public speaking opportunities. In doing so, I was able to lend my personal talents to causes I cared deeply about, in various capacities.

And, because Hometown Health was regarded as a media entity, we earned a valuable opportunity and responsibility to tap into our multimedia platforms to serve as "a catalyst for conversation" (also the slogan of our short-lived monthly print publication).

About three years into the company's development, we established a solid financial foundation. This allowed us the discretion to make impactful contributions through donated or deeply discounted production, expertise, services, sponsorships, or cash donations to community organizations and nonprofits. As I often heard from the executive director of one of the boards I served on, "We all have something to give—time, treasures, or talents."

One year, Dennis McGee, my closest friend from our Leesburg business incubator days who would become an "older brother-from-another-mother," told me his local handyman franchise would be participating in a service day, in which they would be helping to do a variety of projects at a veteran's home. I was excited, asked if he needed any more help, and he welcomed the extra hands. I invited the office to join me and the first question asked was, "Will we be paid our hourly rate?" Since everyone else, including me and the handyman's staff, were volunteering time and some of the materials, shouldn't we all volunteer? Only one of my seven staff members joined me on the job site that day. We worked hard, learned some skills, got dirty, had fun, and were thanked with an abundance of tears, hugs, and a moving level of appreciation from the homeowner.

Me working alongside Dennis (right), making a difference during
"A Day of Service" in support of a local veteran

My inability to get my team to embrace this value was maddening and frustrating. At times, I was even resentful.

As I alluded to in chapter 10 (the first *P*), working to make a difference was one of the core values I had the most difficulty instilling in my staff—or so I thought.

Remember Jenn, the operations manager from a few chapters ago? She was the one who rewired my view of this situation, pointing out something that I had never considered and will never forget.

"Just because they're not participating in the things that are important to you, doesn't mean they're not making a difference. They're making a difference in the things that are important to *them*."

She went on to list, person by person, the things they were involved in outside of the office: their churches, community organizations, animal causes, the environment, and so many other worthy efforts.

While no one would argue that I tried to lead by example, it took me a long time to understand where and how I was failing at integrating this core value into our company culture. I ultimately came to realize that my failure was not recognizing (or, perhaps not being aware) our company members *were* working to make a difference, just not necessarily around the projects that Red Apples Media deemed important.

That year, for the first time, I offered a donation match for all staff who made cash donations to any legitimate local organization. And still, no one took advantage of the offer.

However, even then, I failed to anticipate a few pitfalls in my otherwise well-intended gesture. To begin with, Jenn pointed out to me that some might not want me to know how much they were donating and to whom. For some, those cash donations came from the heart, not for the match. For others, they may not have been able to afford the cash but certainly were generous with their time and talents.

One of the most impactful investments Red Apples Media made in our community was the creation of "The Red Apples Riders" program.

In partnership with a national organization, All Kids Bike, we adopted three of the local elementary schools and, with the support of the local education foundation, purchased twenty-four bikes, helmets, and the licensed training materials for each of the three schools to help elementary kids learn how to ride a bike.

Branded bike helmets for the Red Apples Riders

While every member of my team was involved in what we did—whether designing the "Red Apples Riders" logo, shooting and editing the reveal video, or posting it to social media, I had no illusions or expectations this time around that anyone in the office would care, other than me. In fact, they all clearly took pride in their role and association, unburdened without my typical, self-created expectations.

A client and friend, Joe Ziler, has a personal mantra:

"If you have the ability to make a difference, you have a responsibility to make a difference."[7]

In addition to prioritizing the people and things most important to us, this core value allows you the grace to define your "ability."

You define the difference.
You define its importance.
And above all, you define your motivation to make that difference.

CHAPTER 15

INTERSTITIAL

The Dark Horse, Incorrigible Little Brother

Having left Jacksonville, I arrived in Baltimore at WBAL-TV in the early nineties. It was a significant jump in market size and a big advancement for my career. With it came a chance to live closer to my family in New Jersey, more money, and a more diverse marketplace.

WBAL was a mixed bag for me. In hindsight, it was a time when I was, quite frankly, a handful to manage. I was often told that my talent and creativity was what barely kept me employed. In other words, while I was pushing my boundaries, I was also pushing the buttons of others, simply as a product of being in my mid-twenties. My immediate boss, Kerry Richards, was a good guy who hated confrontation. He did everything he could to guide me, encourage me, and keep me out of trouble.

On one occasion, back in 1993, about two years after joining the station, I called Kerry to come down to the edit suite to approve a promotional spot I had just completed (part of the standard approval process) for an investigative news story about a local health insurance billing scam. I told him, "Leave your shoes and socks in your office. This promo is just going to knock your socks off anyway."

As a union TV station, I had a director and an editor assigned to my production sessions. The dynamic duo of Don Horner (director) and John Dockman (editor) were invaluable, not only in bringing my creative concepts to life, but very often enhancing them. We were a great team, and I had the utmost respect for them both, particularly Don, who seemed to command everyone's adoration and appreciation with his unflappable demeanor, even in the tensest of situations.

Kerry entered the edit suite in his bare feet. "Don't let me down, Marcus," he said in his Texas twang (throughout my career, several coworkers decided to call me Marcus or Marcus Aurelius—I never minded).

As we had hoped, Kerry loved the promotional spot, generously showered accolades on the three of us, and went back to his office to put his socks and shoes back on.

About thirty minutes later, Don answered the edit room phone. It was Kerry giving us a heads-up that the general manager, station manager, and news director were on their way down with Kerry to view the promotional spot.

"This is either going to be really good or really bad," Don said. "I'm going to go with 'really bad.'"

For the few minutes it took for senior management to arrive, the three of us tried to anticipate what we were in for. Just prior to the contingent entering the edit suite, Don advised me, "No matter what, stay professional, and don't lose your composure."

As the four department heads stood and watched the thirty-second promotional spot, John was asked to play it back several times. The general manager thanked us and the four of them left the edit suite.

I was stunned and confused. What just happened? I wanted to believe it was so good that it left them speechless (but not sockless)— a legend in my own mind.

"Wait for it," Don said softly.

A minute later, Kerry opened the door. "Kill it," he said.

"Kill it? I don't understand," I replied.

"It's not for you to understand. We're going to kill the spot."

This was right about the time my brain forgot what Don had advised: "No matter what, stay professional and don't lose your composure."

I did neither. As a matter of fact, I did exactly the opposite of that valuable piece of coaching.

I pushed for more information, claiming my right to know after "pouring my heart and soul" into this creative endeavor, having it approved by the same man who was now telling me to kill it. I demanded an explanation. I was angry, belligerent, combative, and had Kerry not been such a nice guy, he probably would have fired me then and there.

"Kill it. End of conversation," Kerry said, as he walked out of the edit suite.

It was not the end of the conversation in my mind, so I stood up to follow Kerry.

"Sit down and cool down," Don demanded of me in his even-tempered tone. I did. Don probably saved my job that day.

Fortunately, it was a Friday, so everyone had the weekend to calm down.

I would never get a straight answer as to what happened and why the spot was killed. I did get another stern talking-to by the general manager and station manager about how "everyone in the station was rowing in one direction toward success, and it seemed I was determined to row in a different direction, toward my own path to success."

Things became very uncomfortable around the office after that. I couldn't help but feel like all of this could have been handled better, particularly by the management team, all of whom, after all, were many years my professional senior. That was the mindset of a headstrong but creative twenty-something, still evolving and working hard to climb the ladder. It was not one of my prouder moments.

A few weeks after the May "sweeps" rating period came to an end, I caught wind that one of our crosstown competitors, WMAR-TV, was looking for a new creative services director. This was not only my ticket out of WBAL's creative oppression (thought the still headstrong twenty-something), but also a chance to become a manager and not have to move out of Baltimore to do it.

I put together my submission packet and hand delivered it to the WMAR front desk during my lunch hour the next day.

WMAR's general manager, Emily Barr, called to tell me she was already deep in the interviewing process but was intrigued by my résumé and cover letter, and apparently was somewhat familiar with the work I was producing for one of her competitors. She suggested we schedule lunch to meet each other without it being a formal interview.

When we met for lunch, I was immediately drawn in by Emily. She was smart and articulate, strategic and considerate, deliberate and disarming. She also came from a creative background, so I felt that I could not only learn from her, but that she would be sympathetic to the plight of "us creatives." We talked about Baltimore's TV landscape, my background, and observations about the other competitors. Winding down, she asked me if there was anything I could point to creatively that I had recently seen on her station, WMAR, that I would have done differently.

Before I continue, let me give you a very basic education on the significance of February, May, and November, in those days of television stations. Known as "sweeps" periods, these three times of the year were when stations and their affiliated networks put their best content on the air with the goal of earning the highest viewer ratings they could. This effort is for bragging rights, as well as to set the rates for advertising on the stations for the next several months until the next sweeps period. Higher ratings mean more viewers. More viewers mean more eyeballs watching the advertisers' commercials. More eyeballs mean charging the advertisers more.

During the closing days of the May 1993 sweeps, the final episode of *Cheers* had aired on Emily's station. There was guaranteed to be a huge audience watching the finale and a valuable opportunity to pull much of the oversized *Cheers* audience into WMAR's late newscast to boost its ratings. I shared with Emily that I saw the news teaser during the *Cheers* finale and thought it was a missed opportunity in both its production quality and the content.

"Yeah. We had several conversations about that spot the next day," Emily admitted. "Good eye."

As we left the restaurant, she thanked me and told me how much she appreciated chatting with me, but wanted to manage my expectations as a "dark horse, late in the interview process." She would be extending a job offer to someone in the next week or so.

Emily did hire me and it was one of the most influential periods of my career. She was a fabulous mentor, teaching me a great deal about the business, but also how to evolve from a "worker" to a manager, which was no easy task (for either of us).

At one point I was called into her office for something I had done (hard to keep track) and in our conversation about what occurred, she told me that I reminded her of her "incorrigible little brother."

I remember thinking that I should be flattered—that Emily thought of me as family. Until I went back to my office and looked up "incorrigible" in the *Merriam-Webster* dictionary:

> *incorrigible* • \in-KOR-uh-juh-bul\ • adjective. 1: incapable of being corrected, amended, or reformed 2: not manageable[8]

This was clearly not a compliment, leaving me deeply disappointed that I was letting down someone that I truly respected and who had taken a chance on me.

It was a turning point for me. Yes, I would go on to make other mistakes and step on more than my share of land mines in the workplace, but I was slowly growing into the leadership position and its responsibilities, thanks to Emily's patience and guidance.

Emily Barr left WMAR to pursue the first of many extraordinary career opportunities. She went on to become one of the most influential and respected women in modern day broadcasting. Whenever I crossed paths with someone else who worked for or with Emily, either directly or within the station groups she was responsible for, it was always a lovefest of appreciation for the role she played in our respective careers.

She and I continue to stay in touch; the only previous manager I've ever maintained a personal relationship with. She has never refused to let me pick her brain or vent. But she always gives it to me straight, particularly if she knows I will benefit from her candor and counsel.

I still catch myself echoing phrases that were directed at me (sometimes with frustration) by my bosses, including the time—after a large layoff—I had to tell someone, "It's not for you to understand. End of conversation."

That WBAL kill-the-spot experience also helped me coin another Marcism:

"Take pride. Don't take it personal."

The fact is, nothing that happened that day was personal, until I made it personal. I did my job, got paid for it, and people with more authority than me made a decision, for reasons I had no entitlement to. It had nothing to do with me, anything I did wrong (other than how I handled it), or my talents and abilities. Helping creative people separate themselves from their work and "the heart and soul they poured into it" has always been a coaching opportunity.

Finally, I'll admit, after managing hundreds of people during my career, I've called one or two of them "incorrigible."

Thanks, Em.

CHAPTER 16

Extraordinary Is Defined By Actions, Not Words

There is a great deal of hyperbole in marketing. Sometimes the adjectives are specific and definable, such as *first*, or *only*. Other times, they're subjective and open to debate, like *best*, or the *leader*. At Red Apples Media, we wanted to be associated with all of those adjectives, but it was critical that we could back up any claim about what we did and how we did it, as an organization. After all, I believe "extraordinary" is defined by actions, not words.

This was a throwback to a period in which I developed a marketing curriculum using the acronym DRIP (yes, I like my acronyms, and analogies, while we're on the topic).

The *D* in DRIP stood for "differentiation." We would spend a great deal of time taking the client through an exercise designed to shed them of the subjective differentiators, such as "best," "treat you like family," "finest quality," and so forth and instead lock in on definable, quantifiable, and substantiated characteristics that truly differentiate the client from their competition.

It's difficult for you to be taken seriously when you claim to be "the best." That is, *unless* you can quantify it through actions, without reproach, and reposition the claim along the lines of "most award-winning."

One of the promotion managers who worked for me used to say, "I can tell you that I'm a six-foot, four-inch blonde Scandinavian all I want, but as soon as you see that I am a five-foot, eight-inch Italian with jet black hair, I've lost all credibility."

This was specific to the claims we would make in producing television promotional spots for news content, mindful to not create what Ramon Escobar (vice president of news at WTVJ) used to refer to as "anticippointment"—the act of building something up as to create anticipation, only to underdeliver, creating disappointment and a loss of credibility.

We were also firm believers in and strong advocates for letting others proclaim our and our clients' "awesomeness."

We live in a society where reviews and ratings have become critical to everything we do. Chances are you don't shop, hire a contractor, visit a doctor, book a hotel, or go to a restaurant for the first time without looking at reviews. After all, what contractor is going to tell you they are anything but the best? That is why the experiences you provide are so critical to earn powerful, public, positive reviews. Those clients, customers, or patients become your raving fans and your most valuable (and typically, least expensive) source of referrals and new business.

Of course, failure to deliver an extraordinary experience can also create the opposite, negative effect—including low-star ratings and merciless online rants and complaints.

I was intrigued by a seasoned physician client who came to me with an idea. With all the online rating tools available for patients to rate their doctors (good or bad), he wanted to know if we could help him develop a similar rating tool, which would allow doctors a method to warn fellow practitioners about rude, irrational, unrealistic, nonpaying patients, "Fair is fair," he argued. A solid argument, I must admit. Privacy laws and the potential for lawsuits aside, I advised him against it, but suspected he felt better after venting the idea to me.

One of the most challenging situations for a marketer—or a business, more directly—these days is when someone "blasts" you on social media or on a review platform. We have had to advise clients on this countless times over the years. Inevitably, their first reaction is to punch back, which will almost always lead to a counterpunch, and so on.

Recognizing that every situation is specific, in general terms our recommended strategy typically began with a personal outreach to the source of the negative review or comments. Very often, the customer just wanted to get someone's attention, vent, and be heard. If handled correctly, this would often lead to a revised or deleted negative review. We always advised against using the same platform to debate the review with little to gain, other than adding fuel to the fire.

At the same time, we almost always advised a response of some kind, even if it was something along the lines of, "We're disappointed to learn you were not pleased. While we always strive to provide the best experience, we recognize that sometimes that is not possible . . .."

Of course, depending on the specific situation, no reply may be appropriate, or the reply might be customized to strategically lower the heat of the situation.

It is also important to keep negative comments in context with the cumulative body of reviews. In other words, I understand that a single, one-star review can kill your rating when you only have ten reviews. But a one-star review among one hundred positive reviews is much less impactful and will likely be dismissed by potential customers in comparison to the other exceptional reviews you have. There is strength in numbers.

Keeping in mind that you're never going to make everyone 100 percent happy all the time, I would warn clients whose goal was to grow that "the bigger you get, the bigger the target is on you." Whether from competitors, customers, or whomever, there seems to be disturbing and disproportionate joy in taking down success.

What's the answer? Provide such extraordinary actions, interactions, and experiences that any naysayers are drowned out by the overabundance of exceptional support from your most valuable, raving fans.

The ideal situation is to have worked so hard to create a brand that is so beloved and respected, any comment to the contrary would be seen as a "them" problem, rather than a reasonable or realistic reflection on you and your business or personal brand.

Imagine having developed a rock-solid reputation for keeping people's privacy and confidentiality in the things they share with you. Then one day, two people are talking and one accuses you of spreading gossip about something. Wouldn't it be ideal for the other person to stand up and say, "I've known him for years. I have confided in him, have asked for his counsel, and know for a fact those conversations always stayed between the two of us. No way the source of that gossip is from him."

Or, "I've been going to that doctor for years. She is always on time, courteous, and patient with my questions. The negative experience you're describing is so far from the reality I've experienced. I imagine it was either your perception, or there was something more going on. That just seems so out of character."

I've always put a lot of weight in the phrase, "That seems so out of character." It is to suggest that you have developed a level of character that is now part of your brand—personal, professional, or both.

I remember getting a call from a client once, informing me that someone who had just been let go from our company had reached out to warn him that he needed to scrutinize our invoices, alleging we were padding or falsifying our fees. Of course, the idea that a former employee—under any circumstances of separation—would have the gumption (not the word I really wanted to use) to contact a client and spew such falsehoods (also not the word I wanted to use) absolutely infuriated me.

However, the client was quick to talk me off the ledge and immediately made it clear that the longevity of and respect for our relationship gave him no reason to believe that was how I would conduct business. He let me know that he completely dismissed the bogus warning, and called me more as a courtesy heads-up, since he was probably not the only call the former employee had made.

Fortunately, I was not put into a position to defend our team with words, because our actions had already served as a precursor to establishing the extraordinary level of honesty and integrity with which we treated our clients.

Speaking of actions and integrity, one more example of this value comes to mind.

In the mid-1990s, I was offered the chance to return to Jacksonville, this time as part of the leadership team that was starting up the new ABC television station, WJXX. The owners of WJXX had negotiated the ABC affiliation away from WJKS—ironically, the Jacksonville station where I had previously worked.

I found this opportunity to be very appealing, because Jacksonville was where I met my wife and we both really liked it there, so going back would be nice. Plus, it is rare for a new station to launch from the ground up, so being part of that experience was very compelling. Not to mention, they knew I already had experience in the market, and were putting faith in my knowledge of how best to brand and market an unknown entity.

It didn't take long for me to realize I had made a huge mistake. When I first went down to interview, everyone was working out of very nice, rented corporate offices. Not long after, most of us moved out of those plush offices into an old Gap store in a mostly vacant strip mall in a questionable part of town. I used to joke about where various meetings would take place, "In the khakis section, or jeans?"

Yes, I'm being a bit whiny here, but I felt like they had pulled a fast one on several of us. Further, within weeks, I began to butt heads with the news director and other members of senior management, particularly over the branding of the newscasts.

The news director lobbied heavily to brand us as "The First Coast News Leader" (the Jacksonville area is widely referred to as the First Coast).

I argued that we had not yet put a single minute of news originating out of Jacksonville on the air yet (we were producing news content out of a smaller, co-owned sister station in Brunswick, Georgia). To call ourselves "The News Leader" was not only disingenuous, but false by every and any measure.

The news director dug in, making the case that it was important to say it and *then* prove it.

This contradicted everything I had learned up to this point in my career regarding the importance of news integrity. At the same time, it offended my broadcasting, marketing, and professional sensibilities. Mind you, there were already two solid powerhouse news stations in the market, and I felt we would be a laughingstock by adopting that slogan and brand position.

Tension started to build, not just around this battleground, but around others as well. I was beginning to realize that bringing me in to build the brand was not what the owners and my bosses wanted. They had already decided on a brand, which was certainly their right; but had I known, I never would have taken that job, moved, and bought my first house there.

A few weeks later, I was confronted in a department head meeting. The previous evening, one of WJXX's competitors had launched a new marketing campaign, "*The First Coast News Leader.*"

The news director was very aggressive in accusing me, in front of the leadership team, of tipping off some of my past relationships—who still worked at our competitors' stations—that we were building toward that brand (which we had not launched yet).

He speculated that I did this out of spite and to be vindictive, because I didn't get my way in seeking an alternative slogan. Innocent of all his allegations, I got extremely defensive and countered with equal hostility. There was yelling, cursing, and I finally walked out of the meeting, ready to quit.

Here's what happened next.

After a walk around the empty mall to cool off (see, I was learning lessons as I went), I called a friend who was a news producer at the other station.

Me: "Congratulations on the new marketing campaign."

Him: "Thanks. Sorry about that."

Me: "Sorry about what?"

Him: "That we stole it from you guys."

Me: "Stole it, how?"

Him: "Your news set design."

Me: "What are you talking about?"

Him: "Check out the website of the company that's building your news set."

We hung up. I raced back to the computer at my desk to check the website. Sure enough, right on the home page, along with an "Our Latest Work" graphic banner, was the artist rendering of the WJXX news set. Across the front of the main anchor desk in the rendering, in three-dimensional metallic lettering, was "The First Coast News Leader."

Son of a—

I wasted no time calling our station's general manager, having him pull the website up on his computer, with more than just a little (immature) gloating. I demanded he reconvene the group, insisting the news director apologize to me in front of everyone.

Not only did that not happen, but I got fired three weeks later. I was furious, but in my heart, I knew it was for the best. There was no way I could work for an organization hell-bent on branding themselves as something they had not yet taken any action to back it up with.

This experience had a lasting impact on me and has helped guide me through numerous conversations with clients who wanted to brand themselves using superlatives that they had not yet earned.

In some cases, certain actions that make your business extraordinary can also serve as an organic reflection of the organization's character.

As previously mentioned, our investment back into our community was a critical part of what I wanted Red Apples Media to be known for. This was driven by both civic pride and a desire to invest in the things we were most passionate about.

We never did it for awards or recognition, although we received many of both. Some of my best days were those when "the hardware" was delivered to the office. Watching a member of my team tear into the layers of elaborate packaging to reveal his or her Telly Award was always very special to me. We won nineteen Tellys during my tenure. For most staff members, it was their first; others were with Red Apples Media long enough that they won multiple statuettes.

For me, being recognized by peers for our dedication to excellence added another layer to *extraordinary* being defined by *actions*. That third-party acknowledgment provided us the authenticity to claim, with tangible recognition to back it up, that we were, "the area's most award-winning video production marketing company."

My second favorite days were those where we delivered Telly Award statuettes to the clients whose projects garnered Red Apples Media's recognition. Whether wildly accomplished medical practitioners, impactful nonprofits, or blue-collar service companies, the response was always the same. Not only were they astonished that we purchased an additional statuette just for them, they were also moved to be included in the celebration. Most of the clients proudly displayed the statuettes in public view for others to see, fueling ongoing kudos from their guests. Sure, sharing the celebration with the client came from the heart, but it also didn't hurt when they credited Red Apples Media for our award-winning work on their behalf.

The Lake Sumter State College (FL) Lakehawk,
showing off their client Telly Awards

Along with the Telly Awards, others also identified us as being "extraordinary," recognizing Red Apples Media with two Gator 100 Awards (fastest growing businesses founded or run by University of Florida graduates), a Hidden Health Heroes award from the local Department of Health, Entrepreneur of the Year Awards, and several volunteerism awards, to name a few.

There were also a couple of occasions when Red Apples Media nominated clients for national awards without them knowing, until we showed up to present the honor to them. Such was the case with our custom home and roofing clients, both winners of Communitas Awards, for their respective commitment to community causes. In addition to the well-deserved recognition, it built upon their brands and gave us something unique to include in their marketing.

Beyond the awards, we proudly earned a reputation as a local business that was "extraordinarily generous" with its knowledge, resources, willingness to make connections, and even financial support. I made it a point of always trying to invest no less than 3 percent of each year's net revenue back into the community, through services, donations, sponsorships, or volunteerism.

In doing so, Red Apples Media supported health causes; baseball, softball, and fencing teams (I was a high school fencer); animals (mostly dog-related causes, since I'm allergic to cats); the arts; and, most of all, our local public schools, teachers, and students.

There is an old expression, "If you don't toot your own horn, no one is going to toot it for you." Sure, it would be difficult to dispute if I bragged that Red Apples Media was the most generous, philanthropic, connected, and most honored multimedia video production and marketing agency in central Florida.

Instead, I always prefer to let actions lay the groundwork for others to articulate such extraordinary efforts in their own words.

CHAPTER 17

INTERSTITIAL

Fore The Love Of Golf— In The Cold

For all that I came to hate about my job at The Villages, I have to admit that I got to do some incredible things, particularly when I was in good graces during my "Coolness" stretch.

I was an integral part of the team that converted The Villages polo field into a pristine regulation football field for the 2004 and 2005 Villages Gridiron Classic college all-star football game.

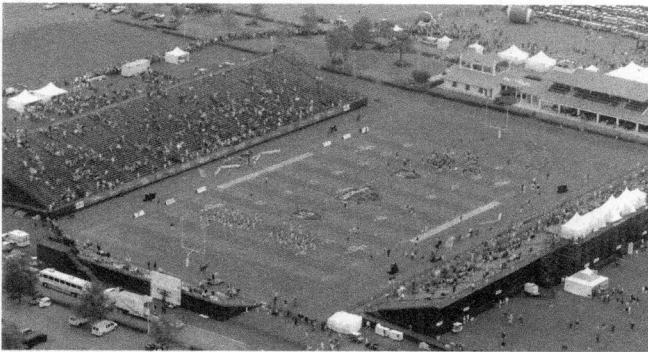

My opportunity to get an aerial view of The Villages polo field, converted into a regulation college football field for the Gridiron Classic

I was part of the group who met with Secret Service in advance of President George W. Bush's—and later, vice presidential candidate Sarah Palin's—visits to "Florida's Friendliest Hometown."

I also hosted Olympic figure skater Brian Boitano, as he toured The Villages and shot segments ahead of a network TV special that I had negotiated the presenting sponsorship for.

I met legendary golfers Arnold Palmer and Gary Player, during separate visits.

I met singers Vince Gill and Amy Grant, as well as iconic New York City radio talk show host Joan Hamburg.

My favorite assignment, by far, was spending time with LPGA golfing great Nancy Lopez.

Nancy had designed a twenty-seven hole golf course at The Villages, with each of the three nine-hole courses named after one of her daughters: Torri Pines, Ashley Meadows, and Erinn Glenn. As part of the relationship, she had a house in The Villages, and also served as its national celebrity spokesperson.[9]

We became very friendly over the years, traveling to pro-am tournaments with Nancy decked out in logo attire. Even her golf bag was embroidered with The Villages logo, for full promotional impact. My role was to maximize The Villages's exposure, but also to make sure Nancy had everything she needed and arrived when and where she was supposed to, and generally serve as her concierge during her appearances. Sometimes we traveled aboard The Villages's corporate jet, other times I drove her, depending on the distance. Either way, we had a lot of time to talk, get to know each other, compare strategies on raising daughters, and delve into whatever else was on her mind.

Mind you, I hate golf. I've never been very good at it, which means I didn't enjoy playing it, which means I was in no rush to play more of it, which means I would never improve, which means I never got any good at it—and the vicious cycle continued.

However, occasionally I would warm up on the driving range with Nancy, as long as I had brought along one of my own left-handed clubs, or the facility hosting any given tournament had one I could borrow.

On one occasion, Nancy and I were warming up at The Villages late in the afternoon, before we would depart early the next morning for one of her pro-am tournament appearances. She was always very kind in offering suggestions about my grip, foot position, follow-though, and other coaching that I always pretended to understand.

Incorporating some of her advice into my next swing, I wound up, followed through, and realized as I did that my arms were moving much faster than usual, and the club was a lot lighter than I had come to expect. I was both stunned and confused for a moment. Meanwhile, Nancy looked over at me, laughing as tears rolled down her face. I remember her kneeling on the ground, laughing uncontrollably—she would later deny that part of the story. Somehow, the entire head of the club had separated from the base of the shaft and was laying on the ground. She claimed that in all her years playing golf, she had never seen that happen. Yay, me.

That oversized club head sits on my shelf with her inscription: "Marc, sorry you lost your head. Nancy Lopez."

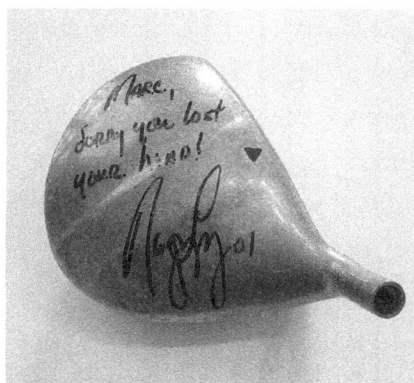

One of my most prized pieces of memorabilia, from LPGA great, Nancy Lopez

At the time, Nancy was married to retired New York Mets third baseman and 1986 World Series MVP Ray Knight. Ray didn't travel with us often, but when he did, I found myself more engrossed in baseball conversation with him, having to be mindful of not ignoring Nancy. Ray was a great storyteller, and I was more than happy to listen to him for as long as he was interested in sharing.

On a chillier-than-usual February morning, the three of us loaded up an SUV, and I then drove us the seventy-five minutes from The Villages to Tampa, where they would both play in the Outback Steakhouse Pro-Am golf tournament the next day.

When we arrived for check-in, we were alerted that start times were likely to be delayed the next morning, due to an overnight cold front moving through. By delaying the tee times, it would allow the course to thaw a little before the first wave of players teed off.

This was of concern for Nancy, as neither she nor Ray had brought the proper clothing to keep them warm enough on the course. "What do you need?" I asked.

"Long underwear," was her reply.

After getting the two of them checked in, I drove over to the Westshore Mall to go shopping.

I realized very early in the outing that I had failed to ask sizes and colors. Not to mention, trying to find long underwear in Tampa (even in February) was not going to be an easy task.

After searching several department stores, I finally found what I was looking for. And then my cell phone rang—it was my wife, Nanci (with an *i*, not to be confused with Nancy, with a *y*, Lopez).

"How are you?" she asked.

"Fine."

"What are you doing?"

"Buying long underwear for an LPGA Hall of Famer and a World Series MVP. You?"

It was (my) Nanci who suggested buying multiple colors and sizes, later returning what wasn't opened nor needed. Which I did, only for the cold front to move through very quickly the next morning and, as I recall, neither wore any of what I bought for them.

Who cares? It still makes for a great story.

CHAPTER 18

Solutions Always Provide More Value Than "No" Or "I Can't"

From the time humans could understand the concept of "No," we resisted it. It carries a negative connotation and almost always puts us on the defensive. Whether you were a toddler who was acting up, a teen who wanted to borrow the car, a young adult who still had a curfew, or a professional who didn't get the raise, "No" was the last thing you wanted to hear. No matter the circumstances, chances are the experience left you with a sour taste, frustration, and at the very least, disappointment. That is, unless the person offering the "No" was creative and compassionate enough to suggest an alternative solution. After all, solutions always provide more value than "No" or "I can't."

This approach became a cornerstone of the RED APPLES way. It was extremely (and I mean, *extremely*) rare that, if we were unable to do something, we didn't have alternative solutions as part of the response. Often, we'd huddle internally to talk through the request and its challenges (time, resources, budget, skills, etc.) so that we were prepared to explain the "No," quickly followed by the "but . . .."

Best case scenario, we were able to deliver some form of the client's request, sometimes even opening their eyes to alternatives they weren't aware of, or hadn't considered. In doing so, Red Apples Media built a reputation for being problem solvers.

Worst case scenario, we got credit for at least trying to bring some level of fulfillment, usually complemented by a variation of, "I appreciate you trying."

Over time, we became a de facto directory of solutions. If someone needed something remotely associated with marketing, production, or community relationships, and weren't sure where to turn, we would get the call or email. Sometimes we could help, and if not, we'd refer them to someone we thought could.

Frankly, being a problem solver or a connector, even if there's nothing in it for us, is probably one of the simpler and most gratifying RED APPLES values. Fortunately for us, most others instinctively regard the extra effort as a burden, quickly dismissing a *Go-Giver* mindset as a waste of time and resources. Their view of these kinds of situational opportunities is typically shortsighted, obscured by the priority of an immediate gain.

On the other hand, we were fueled and energized by the challenge of developing creative and innovative solutions.

Red Apples Media had been working with a hospital client that was getting ready to start building a new wing. They wanted us to "swing by the construction site every couple of days, shoot video, and at the end, put together a montage." Because of the magnitude of the construction project, they let us know they were bidding out this production project to others.

We quickly realized the burden of time this was going to have on our staff and resources over fourteen months (assuming there were no delays). We also factored in the jaw-dropping expense to the client, driven by the frequency of site visits and extensive production. As small and nimble as Red Apples Media was at that time, this was going to be a significant challenge. So, we brainstormed ways to still be able to deliver for this critical, long-time client.

While other production companies came back with proposals in the $60,000–$80,000 range, our proposal was $1,000 per month until the construction was completed—estimated to be around $15,000.

The client called and questioned whether there was a typo in our proposal. I explained that since we didn't have the staffing to do what they were asking, I offered a comparable and significantly less-expensive alternative. I proposed that we set up three mounted, high-definition, weather-safe, time-lapse cameras, which would only have to be checked every two to three weeks, to refresh batteries and memory cards.

We won the production contract with our unique concept, based largely on the credibility we had established as an exceptional steward and partner of this client. Plus, the investment in the equipment was nominal and the impact on our schedule was significantly reduced. Most importantly, the quality (and option of using three camera angles) would make for a final video montage that was reflective of their investment in, and importance of, their strategic expansion.

Our attempt at innovative solutions didn't always go our way, however.

When our local municipality was bidding out management of their public-access cable television channel, Red Apples Media was one of three companies to submit proposals, including the company that had the contract for the past several years.

Because city contracts are public information, we were able to review the details of the current contract, including what the city had been paying. In addition to research showing there was a growing trend toward "cutting the cord" (customers cancelling their cable TV services), viewers were also being drawn in by a plethora of streaming content, rather than seeking out local cable content.

Considering these industry trends, along with my subjective opinion regarding the quality and quantity of content being produced, I firmly believed that the city was overpaying the incumbent provider to operate and produce content for a cable-access channel in the 2020s. It was time to break the outdated compensation model.

Despite some streaming options added for the channel, saving the city and taxpayers money with a proposal that was more in line with the diminishing value and viewership of a local cable-access channel was not only obvious, but responsible.

I took a stab at a proposal that offered our services for *less than the previous budget.* The caveat was that our proposal included a budget of hours per quarter in the form of a "production bank." In other words, the city would have a specific number of hours of video production available ("banked") to use each quarter. The city could use the production bank any way they saw fit, to meet their communication needs. The bank was in addition to scheduled productions—such as city commission meetings—that were shown on the local channel.

In my mind, the incumbent contract was like going to an all-you-can-eat buffet that charges $29 per person, only to realize that you only consumed $20 worth of food had you ordered directly off the menu. That, my friends, is the entire business model of the buffet. But Red Apples Media was not in the buffet business. I knew it would be irresponsible to our overall operations, not to mention a losing financial proposition, to enter into an agreement that had no caps or limitations. Where else in a city budget would you ever get a vendor to agree to that?

"Hello Mr. Car Dealership—we're going to need new police cars."

"How many will you need?"

"As many as we want for $150,000, no caps."

So, rather than saying "No," we proposed an innovative solution that would protect us and cost the city less, while still delivering quantity and quality content. At the same time, it would force the city to be more strategic in what was worth producing, working within their budgeted production bank.

The three proposals were reviewed by a citizen advisory committee. As a follow-up, we were summoned by the committee to a public meeting to answer any additional questions. Red Apples Media scored, by far, the highest in the committee evaluations and would be the recommended provider for the city commissioners to approve at an upcoming vote. I was congratulated, but I knew better.

The incumbent contract holder, furious with the results, started rattling the cages and contacting the commissioners behind the scenes. Mind you, there is nothing inappropriate about doing this—welcome to politics.

The rancor forced the city staff to form a second committee, led by the city manager, to reevaluate the three proposals. Following that committee's review, they reranked the three with the third provider (we'll call them "Ajax Agency" to help you follow the story flow) scoring the highest, followed by Red Apples Media (second), and the incumbent *again* scoring the lowest. The committee of city staff members would recommend the Ajax Agency to the commissioners. It was now the Ajax Agency's turn to be congratulated, but I still knew better. In politics, nothing matters until the final vote is cast.

As you can imagine, the rancor intensified even more. The behind-the-scenes pressure from the incumbent—a tactic I refused to participate in—also intensified, right up until the night of the commissioners' vote. I'll spare you the ridiculous details of how it all played out, other than to say that at the end of the night, the vendor who was ranked lowest of the three by two committees, with the highest proposed budget, won the contract *plus an additional 50 percent* so—as one commissioner put it—"they could do their jobs properly and provide the city the unlimited services they would need."

Most in the room were stunned. I sat quietly, unsurprised and feeling bad for the Ajax Agency, who had already hired people in anticipation of winning the contract, backed by the city staff's recommendation.

My point is, sometimes offering solutions, no matter how valuable, isn't always received the way you might hope, even with the best intentions. If nothing else, we lifted the curtain on this particular group of city commissioners and, in my opinion, one of their most irresponsible decisions of wasted taxpayer dollars in recent memory.

More importantly, in one of the most maddening tests of our values, we stood by ours and what we believed was in the best interest of taxpayers, the city, and our company.

Flashing back to what Jon Stewart said about values, "If you don't stick to [them] when they're being tested . . .."

Or, to share another Marcism:

"The climb is steeper and sometimes
your nose bleeds, but the view
is always better from the high road."

Like anyone, I hate being told "No," especially when I think I'm right. When I am in the position of customer, it is not uncommon for me to use a phrase with a customer service representative along the lines of, "I know you're probably going to tell me you can't help me, but I'm going to give you the chance to create an extraordinary customer experience. Here's what I'd like . . .."

My success in using this approach is fair, at best. It's incredible to me how infrequently businesses even attempt solutions, particularly when you're dealing with call centers that are bound to a script and not empowered to deviate. Or worse, they're penalized for escalating a call.

It was also important to me—and the success of this value—to also empower my team to come up with solutions, particularly when they were on the front line of a situation. In the world of production, few things are worse than, for example, traveling for two hours to a video shoot, only to run into some unexpected or uncommunicated issue. My team would certainly be in their right to turn around and come back. Or, a better, client-centric option, would be to grab an early lunch while the client regroups and then return to the shoot location, so the trip is not a total loss.

No matter the size of your company, or who you're dealing with, even on a personal level (child, spouse, sibling, friend), being a consistent provider of solutions will absolutely differentiate you in a society that is generally wired to just say, "No," or "I can't."

CHAPTER 19

INTERSTITIAL

Missed Opportunities— Or Were They?

I n Darius Rucker's song, "This," he reflects back on both the mundane and important things that didn't work out the way he hoped, all as part of God's larger plan to lead him to "this" better place in his life. [10]

Garth Brooks puts it another way when he sings, with hindsight, in appreciation of God's "Unanswered Prayers." [11]

Generally speaking, the nature of working in television is that you start in a small market (like Bangor), and work your way up to better jobs, better titles, and more money, by moving up to larger markets (like Miami). I had thirteen addresses in the twenty years following college graduation. This also included some moves within the same city, if a promotion afforded me the opportunity for a larger or nicer place to live.

As I look back with a different perspective than I probably had in the moment, the jobs that didn't work out all seem to have been for a reason.

During the summer between my junior and senior year of college, I lined up an internship at WCJB—an ABC station not far from campus—in Gainesville, Florida. When I first called, I asked about a news internship. After being told that those were already filled for the summer, I was asked what else I was interested in. I had been working as a student fundraiser for the University of Florida Alumni Association doing telemarketing, so "marketing" came out of my mouth as an alternative area of interest.

I was put through to the director of promotions, who brought me in for an interview and offered me the internship, but then explained she would be going on maternity leave in a few weeks, during my internship. That internship would set off a string of related events and introductions that set me on the path to becoming a television station promotions and creative services professional. Those began with my first job out of college in Bangor, at a station owned by Hildreth Communications—the same company that owned WCJB in Gainesville.

I didn't join Jim Matthews in Hawaii, but six months later, after leaving Bangor, I would become a member of his staff in Jacksonville, where I would eventually meet my wife Nanci, who was a nightside news producer at the same station.

Some of the best jobs I didn't get now make for the best stories.

For example, back in the day, *Broadcasting & Cable* magazine (commonly referred to as simply *B&C*) was one of the most widely read industry publications. I would eagerly await my weekly issue, check out the announcements of promotions and career changes, and peruse the employment opportunities (pre-internet).

In 1996, a year into the Baltimore affiliation switch—in which we were now an ABC network affiliate—I was "on the rise" among the ABC affiliate and Scripps Broadcasting (who owned the station) creative directors.

Jamie Tarses, daughter of legendary TV writer and producer Jay Tarses, was named the president of ABC Entertainment, the first woman and one of the youngest network executives to hold the role. I recall seeing a *B&C* interview where she shared her desire to build a team of creatives from nontraditional corners of the industry. That was all I needed to read as I developed my plan to get her attention.

Over the course of five days, she would receive an overnight package at her LA offices from my home in Baltimore every day. It was strategic and expensive. Each day's package would be meticulously planned and crafted, mustering a plethora of puns that would put this regional Emmy Award winner on Tarses's radar.

Day one was a pizza box with a letter glued inside explaining how I was going to "deliver unique ideas and creativity" as a member of her team.

Day two was a large box with helium balloons inside; when the box—labeled, "Warning: Contagious Creativity Enclosed"—was opened, the balloons would rise from the box with cheesy puns about "new creative heights."

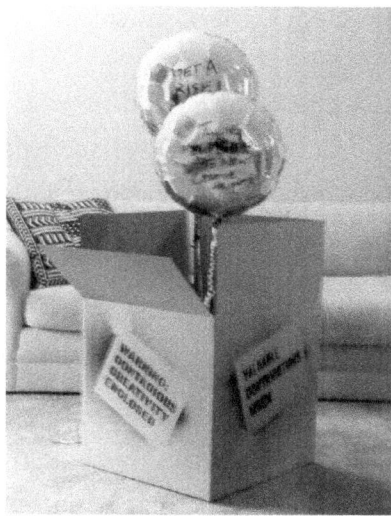

One of the four creative attempts to get the attention of Jamie Tarses

Day three was a baseball bat, shipped in a large poster tube, with a letter making the case that, "as a member of her team, we'd develop hit after hit." You would have thought two puns in one package would score some extra points.

On the fourth day, my phone rang. It was Tarses's assistant, calling to let me know that while they were thoroughly enjoying my deliveries, "Ms. Tarses wanted me to call to let you know she has her team in place and is not hiring at this time. You can stop sending things." I apologized in advance for the next delivery, already in transit, and thanked her for the call. The editors of this book begged me to share what the in-transit package was. Feel free to ask me yourself at a future book-signing or speaking engagement.

A few years later, still "on the rise," but now with an NBC-owned station in Miami, I was invited to interview for a job with the network's creative team in LA. I had become very close with several of the senior staff, and they hinted the job was all but mine if I wanted it. They were so confident, they'd even set me up with a real estate agent to show me around LA before my interview, which was positioned as "mostly a technicality."

The real estate agent picked me up in front of the hotel where the network had put me up the night before. She parked, hopped out to introduce herself, opened the passenger side door of her minivan, and I was immediately hit by one of the foulest odors I had ever smelled. I climbed into the passenger seat, which was wrapped in a lambswool seat covering.

By now, I had identified the unmistakable stink as that of wet dog. Turns out the real estate agent also had show dogs, who liked to ride in the car. In the meantime, the seat covers were fermenting and baking every molecule of the stench. As I adjusted the air vents, foolishly thinking it would make a difference, I began to feel the undeniable bites of fleas on my exposed neck, hands, and arms (fortunately I was wearing jeans).

I can't tell you a single thing about any of the listings we looked at. Distracted, irritated, and itchy, I dreaded every mile, desperate to get back to the hotel and shower before having to rally for the interview. By the way, it was an interview that I bombed so spectacularly that one of my biggest NBC champions followed me out of the meeting room afterward and asked, "What the hell was that? Who did we just interview?"

I remember an extensive interview process to join the Coca-Cola marketing team in Atlanta, making it all the way to waiting for the offer letter. After not hearing anything for a week, I learned the person I would have been reporting to was fired, as was most of the team I had interviewed with.

Travel has always been my indulgence, so when I decided to transition out of television and bring my creative and marketing skills to the travel industry, I was thrilled to be offered a position with Renaissance Cruise Lines—a small, boutique cruise line based out of South Florida. Just days later, before I received the official paperwork, the world was rocked by the attacks of 9/11. Travel would be shut down for weeks, and Renaissance would never resume operations.

My job at WTVJ in Miami also came via a circuitous route. I had been deep into the interview process for the head of creative at the MSNBC London bureau. For reasons I never fully understood, the recruitment was being spearheaded by Mike Pustizzi, the vice president of human resources for WTVJ (both entities were owned by NBC). It had reached a point where I was being warned to prepare for life overseas during a two-year contract. Then, out of nowhere, Mike called and asked if I would have greater interest in Miami, rather than London. WTVJ had parted ways with the vice president of creative services during my MSNBC interview process, and Mike thought I would be an ideal fit.

The timing of this interstitial wasn't an accident. It perfectly sets up the role The Universe played in my life before I was even aware of it and is certainly why it served as the core of the RED APPLES core values.

So, hurry up, turn the page, and let me tell you about a chilly, drizzly night in Baltimore, 2012.

CHAPTER 20

Respect The Universe (For Real, This Time)
The Core Of Red Apples Media's Success

B y now, unless you cheated and skipped ahead, you've been introduced to eight of the nine core values that transformed a company that was "founded out of fear and desperation, into one of passion and purpose."

For me, the most impactful guiding principle was the one I had the least control over, other than the control to relinquish control. *Read that again.*

Respect The Universe.

I spent the better part of my professional career focused on control. This included valiant and exhaustive efforts trying to control my own circumstances, others, situations, conditions, results, and practically every other element of my life. Along the way, I absolutely failed in my effort to control things much more than I succeeded and, without a doubt, alienated people and lost jobs as a costly result.

It wasn't until I began to understand and accept the power of The Universe, developing a personal belief that I represented a mere speck of significance in a larger mechanism that was so far beyond my control and understanding, that my life began to experience a seismic shift.

An evolving respect for The Universe started to take shape shortly after the previously mentioned lunch that led to my reading (and rereading many times) of *The Go-Giver*. While the book's message had nothing directly to do with putting faith in The Universe, it did provide a powerful message about how actions (or inactions) influence larger outcomes.

Some might call this faith in a higher being, karma, serendipity, luck, chance, or, simply, coincidence.

Once I began to actively stop myself in situations that I was trying to control, and then release that control to The Universe, my perspective changed. This also freed me to reallocate my energies to the things that I could at least have some degree of impact on or influence over.

A growing and evolving respect for The Universe led me to a powerful epiphany:

We can only make withdrawals from The Universe
if we're making equal or greater deposits,
without expectation of earning interest.

My watershed experience came between two baseball stadiums.

I'm not as much a fan of baseball as I am of baseball stadiums. Whenever I travel, I always try to catch a game, so I can add another stadium—major league, minor league, college—to my map of visited stadiums. But if I had to pick a team, I would tell you the Baltimore Orioles are my team, dating back to my five years living in "Charm

City" just after Oriole Park at Camden Yards—the crown jewel of Major League Baseball at the time—opened.

Back in May of 2012, I was visiting a friend and client in Baltimore on business. Chris knew there was no way I could come to town and not catch an Orioles game, so she scored four tickets for us and two of her coworkers. As the temperature began to drop and a light rain began to fall, her coworkers bailed on us. We went to the stadium, and I suggested we give the two extra tickets away. I've done this on numerous occasions, and I am always perplexed by those who won't take them, simply because they think there's a catch.

After a few rejections, we found a college-age couple standing in line to purchase tickets and offered our two extra tickets for free.

"What's the catch?" asked the female.

Actually, there was one catch. I never hand free tickets to someone and walk away. They must enter the stadium with us. Not that I doubted their honesty, but I've been burned by some who took the tickets and, I suspect, sold them afterwards.

I'm sure the weather was a significant factor, but Chris and I marveled at how empty the stadium was. Forget the "announced attendance," my guess is that there were no more than a thousand people sitting in the damp, chilly seats. Chris was a trooper.

To our surprise, the couple came and sat in their ticketed seats right next to us—five rows behind the dugout on the third base side. They could have sat anywhere in the stadium, but they chose to sit next to the strangers who gifted the tickets to them. As we chatted, Chris and I learned they were, in fact, college students. It was his birthday, and she had been saving for months to treat him to his first Orioles game. Our free tickets saved her about $190, which she could now use to purchase two desperately needed new tires for her car.

Chris and I were feeling pretty good, and I suggested to her that The Universe connected us to that couple that night.

Here's where it gets interesting.

Since 2004, my friend Mark (with a *k*) and I have enjoyed a "Guys Baseball Weekend." Every summer for fifteen years, we picked a city, arrived on Friday, and came home on Sunday. The purpose is simple: visit a stadium (or in some cases, multiple stadiums, if the major league cities were close enough, such as Houston and Arlington) and enjoy the architecture, the unique nuances and traditions of each stadium, the food, beer, fans, and the game.

In July of 2012, two months after my visit to Baltimore, Mark and I visited PNC Park for a Pittsburgh Pirates game. This was a rare occasion, in which we didn't have tickets for the game. For the most part, each year I was usually able to secure tickets through my extensive media and marketing network. On this trip, we would have to do it the old-fashioned way: buy them at the ticket window.

I purposely selected the hotel based on their "game-day convenience shuttle" to and from the stadium for ten dollars each, round trip. To me, it beat driving, parking, and traffic. We had gotten really good at the strategies of our baseball weekends.

Mark and I headed down to the lobby two hours before the first pitch to get the first shuttle. I like to get to the stadium early, watch batting practice, and scout the food. Plus, we still had to buy tickets. We waited for thirty minutes without a shuttle coming to the hotel. As we continued to wait, the crowd of people who had the same plan began to grow. A quick mental headcount strongly suggested more people were waiting than the first shuttle would hold and it occurred to me, when the shuttle did come, there would be a mad, physical dash to get on. I really had no interest in dealing with that and suggested to Mark that we check to see if we could get a refund for the shuttle tickets, then try to find some kind of public transportation option. My anxiety was building.

Following the vague directions from the teen at the hotel's front desk, we drove to what we thought was a public parking lot for a shuttle bus to the stadium. We parked the car and began to follow the crowds, who were dressed in Pittsburgh black and yellow. We reached a kiosk, not for a bus, as it turned out, but a ferry, to take game attendees across the Allegheny River to the stadium for fifteen dollars each, round trip. Are you kidding me? So, not only did we lose more time and pay for parking, but now we've increased our transportation costs to the stadium by 50 percent. My frustration was growing while my patience was diminishing.

I tried to convince Mark that we should walk away out of principle, but he convinced me otherwise.

We paid, boarded the ferry, and waited for more than thirty minutes. I never understood why we waited so long, but it was tormenting to see the stadium just on the other side of the river. My foot started to tap. My head started to pound. I was keenly aware of my physiological response to the situation and growing concerned about our ability to get tickets (I had written off batting practice by now).

The unique and picturesque (if not annoying) ferry approach to PNC Park

Mark, sensing my agitation, suggested, "You know this is The Universe screwing with us."

I snapped back, "Don't you dare play The Universe card with me! This is just BS, plain and simple."

I'll admit, once the ferry departed the dock toward the stadium, it was a pretty cool view as we approached the stadium docks from the river. It would definitely be one of our most unique and memorable baseball stadium arrivals. Unfortunately, at the time, I was too distracted and consumed by the anger that had built over the two hours since we had first left our hotel room to catch the ten-dollar "convenience shuttle."

When the ferry docked, we realized it had left us on the absolute farthest side of the stadium from the main ticket office, except for a single ticket window near where we stood. There, the ticket window attendant informed us they only had standing-room tickets remaining. I was now consumed by the real possibility that after all of this, we might not get into the game. I convinced Mark we should split up and look for anyone selling tickets.

Out of the corner of my eye, I saw two college-age guys chatting up some tickets with a female fan around their age. When she waved them off and walked away, I approached him. "Extra tickets?" I asked.

"Yeah. Two."

"How much do you want for them?"

One looked at his friend and they shrugged. He replied, "Well, a friend of my dad's gave them to us, so I don't really feel right charging you for them."

"That would be great. Maybe let me buy you guys a beer?"

"We're not old enough to drink, but thanks. But we're kind of ready to head in and I don't want to just give you the tickets and walk away. Do you mind walking in with us? Nothing personal."

I felt my entire demeanor change. The anger that must have been embedded in my facial expression began to soften and my blood pressure headed back toward normalcy. Almost word for word, this young man put the same requirement on the free tickets as I did two months earlier in Baltimore.

We found Mark and the four of us walked through the turnstiles together. I leaned into Mark, "You're not going to believe this. I'll explain when we sit."

We thanked the two young men and told them we'd see them at the seats.

Mark and I stood in the beer line, recapping our past two hours. I began to piece together how all of these indisputable annoyances and detours, in fact, led us to two free tickets. Had we taken the shuttle, had we found the correct commuter lot with the bus, had we not swallowed our pride and boarded the ferry, had the ferry not sat as long as it did, and, had the ferry not docked where it did, would any of this have happened? As Mark said, sometimes The Universe just likes to screw with you.

With food and beverage in hand, we found our section of the stadium. As we got closer, my eyes began to widen, and my heart began to beat faster. We were on the third base side. We walked down our aisle and found our original guys. Mark and I sat next to them, *five rows behind the dugout.* Not *exactly* where I had sat in Baltimore a few months earlier, but within twenty feet. Which goes to show, even The Universe isn't perfect.

Back then, Oriole Park at Camden Yards had a seating capacity of nearly forty-six thousand, while PNC Park had a capacity of just over thirty-eight thousand.[12] And yet, The Universe seemingly brought us to near identical seats, under extremely similar circumstances, two months apart from otherwise independent events.

I have dozens of examples of how and when The Universe affected the course of my life, but I typically turn to the baseball tickets example to best exemplify its presence.

Say what you want about that story. Scoff if you'd like.

I honestly don't know to what degree anyone who came to work for me truly believed in and adopted my belief. Regardless, they certainly heard me attribute countless situations and results to The Universe. If nothing else, they respectfully played along.

It was only many years after the fact that I understood The Universe had been teeing me up to part with The Villages before I got laid off in 2008.

What I perceived to be critical hires, lucrative opportunities, desired contracts, sought-after potential projects, and clients that fell through: The Universe.

Similarly, we had clients leave us, sometimes even sticking us with unpaid invoices (rarely, but still), and I acquiesced to The Universe. Inevitably, nearly every time, we'd learn that we were better off.

Competitors would turn to infuriating, unprofessional tactics, trying to distract us from staying on our course to success, or "to swing at pitches in the dirt." We held our ground, often fighting against our emotions and what we thought was common sense. Inevitably, The Universe almost always caught up to those competitors, as well.

Sometimes, after a full day of work, we would drag ourselves to a community event that we desperately didn't want to go to. Finding a way to pass the time, we'd strike up small-talk conversation with a stranger, leaving the event feeling as if it was a huge waste of our evening. Then, months later, we'd get a call from that same stranger, wanting to connect us to a friend who was in need of Red Apples' talents and services.

A big part of respecting The Universe is not always recognizing when it's affecting you. I have several very close friends with whom I've discussed this mindset, and some will fight me every step of the way. At the most extreme, some have lost children or spouses to premature death, and are furious with The Universe (if they believe in it at all). I understand to the degree that I am able, having not experienced that kind of trauma. Surely, they would trade any plan The Universe had in mind to get those loved ones back.

In business and in life, everything we want to happen will not always go our way. Very often, with open eyes, an open heart, and a leap of faith, on a timeline determined by The Universe, the reasons will inevitably present themselves.

My final thought on "Respecting The Universe" is that there are three nonnegotiable rules that I have identified over time:

---

1. **You can't negotiate with The Universe.** No matter how hard you try to offer promises, sacrifices, offerings, or deals, The Universe is deaf to those tactics. That said, as I mentioned before, I do believe The Universe provides "dividends" to those who make selfless, organic "deposits" without expectation (a theme explored in *The Go-Giver*).

2. **You can't time The Universe.** The Universe works on its own timeline. No matter how badly you want to land that job in a timeframe that is important to you, it's out of your hands. No matter how important that new client will be to your quarterly goals, The Universe doesn't have key performance indicators (KPIs) to meet.

3. **You can't beat The Universe.** I have been in situations that I sensed were being driven by The Universe, and consciously took actions, said things, or attempted to manipulate the playing field, with the belief that I could alter the inevitable outcome. Quite frankly, it was a waste of my time and energy. I've never been able to alter the inevitable.

Over the years, I've collected photos of like-minded references to The Universe. For example, this interpretation, which is found on a handcrafted piece of wall art at a New Jersey farmers market:

The Universe sends us exactly what we are ready for
at the exact time we need it in our lives.

Or this reminder from a plaque in the sidewalk outside the New York Public Library, which reads:

The Universe is made of stories, not of atoms.
—Muriel Rukeyser[13]

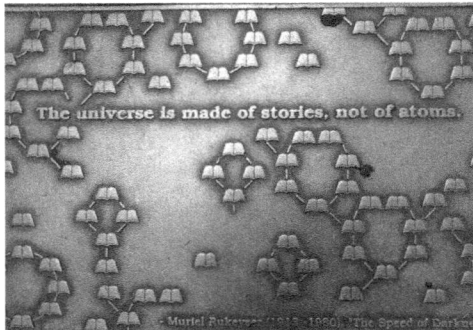

I've even found references in the most unlikely of places—a fortune cookie:

First learn to "give" and then the universe will reward you.

As I mentioned early on, "Respect The Universe" is the most difficult of the RED APPLES core values to wrap your mind around. It took me years to identify it, understand it, and adopt it. And there are still times when I recognize that I have slipped back into "control mode."

Respect for The Universe requires extraordinary self-confidence. It demands constant vigilance, awareness, and the willingness to allow life to play out, even when it seems counterintuitive or at odds with what we believe we want and need at that moment in time.

This is not to say that we don't have any influence over our lives and should just go about life passively and aimlessly. But respecting The Universe means having a deep, personal understanding that we have much less control than we thought, let alone are probably comfortable with.

Then, finding peace with that realization.

CHAPTER 21

Marc's Final Remarks

I didn't initially intend to refer to myself in the third person in naming this chapter. It's a bit of a throwback to when I used to write Marc's Remarks, a column for a local magazine published by Red Apples Media. Plus, I like the alliteration.

You can credit, or blame, genetics. When I was thirteen years old and became bar mitzvah, my extremely creative mom—who oversaw all the baseball theming and decor for the celebration—referred to my table of closest friends as *The ReMARCables*. My mom will never miss a chance for a pun or a play on words—no matter how much we beg.

My mom and dad at my Bar Mitzvah,
playing up the ReMARCables theme

And, whenever I would receive a kind compliment about some marketing idea, I would remind people, "You can't spell marketing without Marc—You'd *misspell* it, but still."

In late 2024, I completed the sale of Red Apples Media, exactly fifteen years and six months after we incorporated Hometown Health TV, LLC. This was not an easy decision, but as I have been reminded by many, it's the storybook entrepreneurial dream. Start a business, build it up, make an impact, create value, and sell it to someone who will hopefully continue to grow it and perpetuate the legacy.

I began the process two years prior, shortly after coming out of the COVID-19 pandemic. As I previously shared, this was a period during which I was feeling exhausted and unappreciated. While Red Apples Media continued to remain profitable during the pandemic—in large part because we were nimble and able to pivot to related service offerings that were in demand at the time—we certainly saw an understandable drop in our profitability.

Like many "lone wolf" entrepreneurs I've spoken with over the years, I was the one who started the company, became its "face," and remained the only constant throughout its history. I developed a growing concern that I had painted myself into a corner, becoming so closely associated as the brand of Red Apples Media. Who would want to buy Red Apples Media if I was no longer associated with it? Further, would we lose clients and staff if I wasn't at the helm?

Yes, there is some ego in this way of thinking, but also a lot of reality. I've seen it play out both ways when clients would sell their businesses. Some would walk away and never look back, while others were begged to come back in some capacity after the sale.

Ideally, one or a few members of my longtime staff would have wanted to buy the company they helped build, but I knew that wasn't going to be an option. I had great soldiers working for me, none of whom I believed had the interest (or finances) to take on the demands of ownership. Not long after I had started to think about a sale, I was driving with my most senior staffer who flat out asked me what my exit strategy was. This caught me off guard, but I already knew the answer. I explained that I saw three potential scenarios:

- One or a group of you buy me out.
- Someone else buys Red Apples Media.
- I decide I'm done, thank you all, collect your keys, and close up shop.

I don't think, at the time, any of those scenarios brought him any comfort, but I was honest when asked.

Anyway, back to the timeline.

When I made my first confidential contact with a business broker in early 2022, and shared some preliminary financial information, he encouraged me to hang in there for another eighteen to twenty-four months. He explained we'd be better positioned for sale if I could get the post-COVID-19 profitability back to prepandemic levels, to show the company's resilience and forward momentum. Otherwise, he feared a potential buyer might use the dip to lowball an offer.

I understood, and hunkered down with some very specific goals in mind:

- *Drive revenue* by actively recruiting quality clients whose needs would tap deeply into the Red Apples Media offerings, shifting our focus to reduce the number of smaller, one-time projects. A cryptic number was written on a whiteboard in my office, so I knew the quarterly revenue target I was aiming for.
- *Manage costs* without adversely affecting the staff or the overall organization. One of my bosses at my first job in Jacksonville used to refer to this as differentiating *nice dos* versus *need dos*.
- *Clean up the staff*, eliminating any drag on the team, and replace them with people who were more aligned with Red Apples

Media's values and objectives. It had only taken one employee, who ultimately beat me to the punch by resigning, to completely change the mood and dynamic of the team. This was entirely my fault. I settled for too long and failed to step up to the decision that should have been made much sooner.

- *Commit to stepping back and being more deliberate in delegating to staff* much earlier, so they had more direct and immediate interaction with clients, particularly the new ones. It was a tricky balance, especially with longtime clients. I was very cognizant of making sure they never felt or perceived that I was no longer engaged, or had "downgraded" them to pursue "shiny new objects."

- *Do all of this under the strictest of secrecy*, while treating every day and every project as if nothing was going on behind the scenes. This was a tactic I learned from one of my clients, who caught me completely off guard when they sold their four-generation family business and explained that, up until the last possible minute, only the husband and wife who owned the company, along with one senior employee, knew what was in the works. Even their own adult children were in the dark until it was official. After all, both of our businesses were in "a small town with big ears and bigger mouths," as I had often observed. Mine was a very small "cone of silence," which included me, my wife, and the broker, until the last possible minute.

- *List the business for sale in early 2024.*

Red Apples Media signed a listing agreement, and the "blind," unnamed listing went live in March 2024. We had several inquiries—even a few confidential virtual interviews—with prospective buyers. I decided early on that finding the right person, with the right motivation, who believed in our successful approach and values, was nonnegotiable. Yes, I wanted a maximum return. But I also put a critical amount of weight on the buyer's character.

None of the initial buyers interviewed aligned with that objective.

In May, we were traveling as a family, celebrating our daughter's college graduation, when I received a text from the broker: "I know you're on vacation but I need to talk to you. Please call me when you have a moment."

We had just pulled into the parking lot of a restaurant for breakfast. I sent my wife and daughter ahead and told them I had to make a quick call.

As I paced the parking lot, the agent let me know we had a full-asking-price offer from someone who had not even hit our radar prior to the offer. That said, it was clear from this conversation that the potential buyer had done a great deal of research in preparing to make his offer. We agreed to proceed with the preliminary paperwork and to set up a meeting when I was back in town.

While I was on the call, my wife texted me about our very astute daughter: "She knows something is up and is worried. Be prepared."

We had breakfast and then drove for several hours as if nothing had happened. Meanwhile, my head was spinning with rational and irrational thoughts, my stomach in knots. Could it really be this easy? A full-asking-price offer in less than ninety days? Did I set the asking price too low? Was I making the right decision?

To put your mind at ease, we let our daughter into the "cone of silence" later that afternoon. Swearing her to secrecy, I explained to her that she was now the sixth person on earth who knew what was happening. We had also brought in my brother by then, who is our financial advisor. My parents were still unaware, mostly so I could avoid an onslaught of well-meaning questions for a little longer.

If this were a movie, you'd be watching a short music montage to creatively advance you through space and time—while I skipped a whole lot of details—advancing you to the takeaway from the experience.

I've often referred to the buyer as "the right guy, at the right time, with the right offer." When I returned from my trip and arranged to meet him in person—after the Red Apples Media office had closed and the staff all went home—I quickly developed a sense of comfort that our values were very much in alignment. Already impressed with the research he had done, I felt he also asked great questions, showed genuine interest in the people he would be inheriting and the client relationships we had developed, and was generous in sharing his vision of Red Apples Media's next chapter.

As a side note, my wife, Nanci—who stalked the buyer's online profile—made the observation that he looked very much like her deceased father, in his younger years. We later learned the buyer grew up not far from the village in Poland that my father-in-law was from before being sent to a German work camp during World War II. Nanci and I both believe her father would have been overjoyed with how this was all playing out and that The Universe was his vehicle for lovingly sticking his nose into my transaction.

After closing the deal ninety days after the offer (that was six months from listing to sale!), the new owner and I coordinated the announcement to the staff. I would share the news with them during our weekly staff meeting and he would come in to meet everyone about two hours later. Following some stunned reactions, a few tears, and assurances that I worked very hard to make sure I was leaving them in good hands, our next critical mission was to personally introduce the new owner to Red Apples Media's clients, vendors, and community partners, assuring them of a seamless transition.

I stayed on during a thirty-day or so transition and quickly realized it was time for me to get out of the way, so the new owner could begin to put his own mark on Red Apples Media. He and I continue to have a great relationship and stay in touch as needed, and he appears to have stayed true, as best I can tell, to following the RED APPLES way.

Sure, I will occasionally hear from a client, or someone in the community, letting me know, "It's just not the same over there without you." I think in most cases they're just being courteous, but it's kind and flattering, just the same.

When I look back on the legacy of those fifteen years, I think of all the people who came to work at Hometown Health TV and Red Apples Media. Each brought their own personality and left their own mark. While some were poor hires on my part, I have great respect and appreciation for others and the roles they played, the skills they developed, the lessons they both learned and taught, and the numerous awards and accomplishments we achieved together.

Just a few of the 19 Telly Awards honoring Red Apples Media for its creative excellence

I reflect on the lasting impact we had, leading with our actions as community advocates in support of public education, health and wellness, mental health, fellow small businesses, and youth sports, to name just a few. Similarly, I take great pride in the role Red Apples Media played in helping many of our clients incorporate our community into their own brand, committing to causes that aligned with their specific core values, and their own desire to make a difference.

I take immense pride in our innovation, strategic and calculated risk-taking, and the standards we set, forcing those who wished to compete to rise to our standards or fizzle out.

I marvel at the times we were tested, and by staying true to our values, prevailed much more often than failed.

I have a high level of paternal pride in now sitting back and watching Red Apples Media 3.0 (I count post-COVID-19 as 2.0) build toward continued success, adapting and interpreting the core values that formed its foundation and led it to become a company that was desirable for someone else to purchase.

Finally, I have great appreciation for the relationships I developed, particularly those who became personal friends, because, whether they realized it or not, they shared a belief in many of these core values.

To remind you, there are nine of them. And as I said in the first chapter, if you can adapt or adopt at least five of them into your business, and perhaps even your life, I think someday that you, too, will step back with a great degree of pride, knowing you had gleaned and benefited from *The RED APPLES Way*.

And if absolutely nothing else, at least now you know how to properly pronounce Bangor.

You're welcome.

The RED APPLES Way

Respect The Universe.

Excellence In Everything. Period.

Deliver On Commitments.
Overdeliver On Expectations.

Anticipate Client Needs And Opportunities.

People Are Our Priority.
Relationships Drive Success.

Profits Are A Function Of Integrity,
Not Sales.

Live For What You Love.
Work To Make A Difference.

Extraordinary Is Defined By Actions,
Not Words.

Solutions Always Provide More Value
Than "No" Or "I Can't."

Acknowledgments

Anyone who knows me knows my passion and preference for handwritten thank-you notes. In addition to the deep personal experience of receiving something in the mail, the never-ending flow of daily electronic communications makes this simple effort even more impactful. For those with whom I've already shared such appreciation, here's a little more.

Throughout this book, I acknowledge the dozens, if not hundreds, of people that I worked with who played various roles throughout my career. Some by name, some more generically; some are very aware, some probably have no idea, and others have since passed.

And while a bit cliché, it all began with my parents, Joyce and Stu, who truly set the tone for what would become my work ethic—albeit, with me kicking and screaming during much of my youth. I also want to express deep appreciation to my brother, Chet, who not only provided valuable financial guidance throughout the sale of Red Apples Media, but more importantly, introduced his big brother to a life-changing curriculum at a critical time in my career, redirecting me away from a self-destructive professional path by embracing a life driven by integrity and accountability.

My thanks to Bob Morris for helping me initially navigate publishing, and to Ryan Harcher and Loren Vasquez, who were among the first to review the manuscript and provide invaluable feedback and encouragement. Also, thanks to Carolyn Maue and Ann Bowers-Evangelista, who both led me to Henry DeVries, along with Devin DeVries, Mike DeTuri, Jazmin Barnes, and the incredible team at Indie Books International. I am honored to be a member of the Indie Books International family and greatly appreciate the expertise and patience in bringing this venture to fruition.

To everyone who ever came to work at Hometown Health TV and Red Apples Media—whether you lasted a week (yes, we had a couple of those) or ten years and counting—know that you all left an impression and either taught or reinforced important lessons for me along the way.

To you the reader, thank you for the generosity of your time and interest in my cocktail hour stories and the RED APPLES way.

Thank you to my wife (and editor of the first four drafts), Nanci, who has stood by me at every turn, every job change, every change of address, every creative endeavor, and every setback. I was traveling when I won my first Emmy Award, back in 1993, so Nanci went to the ceremony to accept it for me. After thanking the usual suspects, I later heard she ended the acceptance speech with "and he'd probably want to thank *me* for all of *my* love and support." I couldn't have said it better myself—then, or now.

Finally, to "The Kid," my Little Love. Thank you for being so flexible, coachable, and encouraging over the years. I wake up every day striving to make you proud, and I hope this book continues to help achieve that goal.

My girlfriend—now wife—Nanci accepting my first EMMY award while I was at conference

Me and "The Kid" inside the 9/11 Memorial subway station in NYC

About The Author

Raised in New Jersey (Turnpike Exit 8a or 9, depending on whether you're coming from the north or south), Marc Robertz-Schwartz is a multi-award-winning media and marketing executive and entrepreneur.

After graduating from the University of Florida, he spent the first twenty years of his career working in creative services, sales, and marketing positions for television stations along the East Coast, from Maine to Miami. Following an economy-driven layoff in 2008, he founded the start-up Hometown Health TV, LLC, an innovative, subscription-based, monthly health and medical marketing video magazine, producing more than 150 consecutive monthly episodes, garnering more than two dozen industry and community honors and awards.

The company would later rebrand as Red Apples Media, reflecting a broader base of full-service marketing agency services, leading to continued year-to-year revenue growth until Marc closed on the sale of the agency in late 2024.

With his extensive on-air video, radio, podcast, and live-event experience, Marc helped raise in excess of $1 million—as emcee and auctioneer of countless events—with a focus on supporting medical, educational, and other community-based causes.

Among numerous honors for both his marketing and entrepreneurial endeavors, Marc is a three-time regional Emmy Award winner and nineteen-time Telly Award winner; was twice named to the Gator 100, for fastest growing companies owned by UF graduates; and was named the International Incubator Business of the Year in 2012, by the National Business Incubation Association.

A lover of travel and dogs, a seeker of craft breweries, and a master of eighties music and movie trivia, he currently lives in central Florida with his wife, Nanci, and is a devout "daughter dad."

For more information about consulting, speaking engagements, bulk book orders, or to share your favorite craft brewery, please visit TheRedApplesWay.com or scan the code.

Endnotes

1   "Frequently Asked Questions," The Villages, accessed August 13, 2025, https://www.thevillages.com/faq/.

2   "Record Number of Pets Enter Hawaii," NBC News, June 28, 2004, https://www.nbcnews.com/id/wbna5317837.

3   Mike Bianchi, "Firing Dan Mullen Is not the Answer for the Gators—Yet," *Orlando Sentinel*, updated November 8, 2021, https://www.orlandosentinel.com/2021/11/08/firing-dan-mullen-is-not-the-answer-for-the-gators-yet-commentary/.

4   Bob Burg and John David Mann, *The Go-Giver: A Little Story About a Powerful Business Idea* (Penguin UK, 2010).

5   "Jon Stewart Quotes—Departing Daily Show Host's Best Lines," *The Week*, February 11, 2015, https://theweek.com/tv-radio/62501/jon-stewart-quotes-departing-daily-show-hosts-best-lines.

6   *Apollo 13*, directed by Ron Howard (Universal Pictures, 1995).

7   Kevco Builders, *Kevco Builders Supports LifeStream Behavioral Center*, posted April 26, 2018, YouTube, 2 min., 49 sec., https://www.youtube.com/watch?v=Ykf_mDorD9g.

8   "Incorrigible," in *Merriam-Webster Dictionary*, September 4, 2025, https://www.merriam-webster.com/dictionary/incorrigible.

9   "Lopez Legacy—Clubhouse," The Villages, accessed October 10, 2025, https://www.golfthevillages.com/championship-golf/clubhouse.asp?course=LOPEZ%20LEGACY.

10   "This," by Darius Rucker, track 1 on *Charleston, SC 1966,* Capitol Records, 2010.

11   "Unanswered Prayers," by Garth Brooks, track 7 on *No Fences*, Capitol Records, 1990.

12   "Ballpark Comparisons," Ballparks of Baseball, accessed October 10, 2025, https://www.ballparksofbaseball.com/capacity.htm.

13   Muriel Rukeyeser, "The Speed of Darkness. Or Wise Words: The Universe," 1971, as shown on Laurel, Annotated, https://laurel-annotated.com/2017/07/26/the-universe.

List Of Trademarks

49ers® and Niners® are registered trademarks of Forty Niners Football Company, LLC
ABC® and WABC® are registered trademarks of American Broadcasting Companies, Inc.
All Kids Bike® is a registered trademark of Strider Education Foundation, Inc.
Arnold Palmer® is a registered trademark of Arnold Palmer Enterprises, Inc.
Baltimore Orioles® and Oriole Park at Camden Yards® are registered trademarks of Baltimore Orioles Limited Partnership (L.P.)
BBC® is a registered trademark of British Broadcasting Corporation
Black Entertainment Television (BET)® is a registered trademark of Black Entertainment Television, LLC
Buccaneers® is a registered trademark of Buccaneers Team, LLC
CBS® is a registered trademark of CBS Broadcasting, Inc.
Cheers® is a registered trademark of CBS Studios, Inc.
Coca-Cola® is a registered trademark of the Coca-Cola Company
Covenant Roofing and Construction® and The Difference is The Promise® are registered trademarks of Covenant Roofing & Construction, Inc.
Ed Block Courage Awards® is a registered trademark of Ed Block Courage Award Foundation, Inc.
Emmy® is a registered trademark of The National Academy of Television Arts and Sciences, Inc.
ESPN® is a registered trademark of ESPN, Inc.
Ferris Bueller's Day Off® is a registered trademark of Paramount Pictures Corporation
Florida Marlins® is a registered trademark of Marlins TeamCo, LLC
GAP® is a registered trademark of GAP (APPAREL), LLC
Gary Player® is a registered trademark of Black Knight Trust
General Electric® is a registered trademark of the General Electric Company
General Hospital®, Good Morning America®, One Life to Live®, and School House Rock® are registered trademarks of American Broadcasting Companies, Inc.
Girl Scouts® is a registered trademark of Girl Scouts of the United States of America
Good Morning America® is a registered trademark of American Broadcasting Companies, Inc
Google® is a registered trademark of Google, LLC
Hometown Health® is a registered trademark of Hometown Health TV, LLC
Jeopardy® is a registered trademark of Jeopardy Productions, Inc.
Kansas City Chiefs® is a registered trademark of Kansas City Chiefs Football Club, Inc.

www.ingramcontent.com/pod-product-compliance
Lightning Source LLC
Chambersburg PA
CBHW031854200326
41597CB00012B/409